FORT KNOX
FORTRESS IN MAINE

By
JOHN E. CAYFORD

WITHDRAWN

CAY-BEL PUBLISHING CO.

FORT KNOX

Fortress In Maine

Copyright, 1983.© John E. Cayford

Library of Congress CC No. 83-71723

ISBN 0-941216-10-1

Manufactured in the United States

by

Cay-Bel Publishing Co.

K-91

OTHER BOOKS BY THE AUTHOR

Underwater Work, Cornell Maritime Press, 1959

Skin & Scuba Diving, Fawcett Books, Inc., 1963

Underwater Logging, Cornell Maritime Press, 1964

Underwater Work, 2nd Edition,Revised, CMP, 1967

Diving In Constrcution Operations, USN-NSC, 1965

Penobscot Expedition, C & H Publications, 1975

Maine Firsts, C & H Publications, 1976

Maine Firsts, 2nd Edition, C & H, 1980

All About Maine, Cay-Bel Publishing, 1981

Maine Firsts, 3rd Edition, Revised & Enlarged,
    Cay-Bel Publishing Co., 1983

Fort Kxox - Fortress In Maine, Cay-Bel, 1984

Maine's Hall of Fame, Vol. 1, Cay-Bel, 1987

SOON TO BE PUBLISHED

Maine's Hall of Fame, Vol. 2

Penobscot Expedition, 2nd Ed. Revised & Enlarged

DEDICATION

To

Those hearty souls, both military and civilian, who designed and constructed beautiful Fort Knox,

And To

Ordnance Sergeant Leopold Hegyi, USA

1832 — 1900

The lone guardian who spent 13 long and lonely years as the Fort Keeper at Fort Knox. It is sincerely hoped that this little volume will forever perpetuate his memory.

CAY-BEL PUBLISHING desires to present books to the reading public that are satisfactory in artistic possibilities and physical qualities. **CAY-BEL** gives careful attention to all technical details, design and manufacture.

CAY-BEL will adhere to those laws of quality, thereby assuring a good name and good will.

Viki G. Baudean

Publisher.

CONTENTS

LIST of ILLUSTRATIONS

ACKNOWLEDGEMENTS

Little did I realize when I began the research on Fort Knox that it would have turned into such a work. I felt were I lucky enough I would be able to gather sufficient material to produce a 12 page booklet. Now the research is over and I find more than 100 pages of typed text plus numerous photographs and line drawings about one of the outstanding 19th Century military fortifications in the United States, — and certainly the finest military installation in the State of Maine. I am indebted to many people and agencies who assisted me in preparing this book. I wish to acknowledge the major contributors at this time.

I want to express my deep appreciation to former Maine Parks Commission Historian John Briggs, and my good friend, the late Charles Bradford, former Supervisor of Historical Sites, Maine Parks Commission, for their generous help which made much of this book possible.

Dick Dyer of Bucksport and Winthrop was also most generous in allowing me the use of his volumous collection of data about Fort Knox. It is without doubt that Dick is the most knowledgeable person in the United States concerning every aspect and phase of Fort Knox, its construction, its people, the military personnel, and its numerous anecdotes.

Dick's book will be the most complete documentation of Fort Knox ever written when he brings it to a conclusion.

Departments and agencies of our Federal Government as well as state agencies, libraries, museums, historical societies and individuals have contributed in the production of this book. It would be a long, long list, yet I wish to thank all who assisted in digging out one hundred year old and older documents to make this book as factual as humanly possible.

A personal thanks to my friend Senator Bill Cohen and his Bangor District Office Manager, Mrs. Jacqueline MacDermott, for their help in obtaining a copy of General Seth Eastman's beautiful painting of Fort Knox (1871). The original hangs in our Nation's Capital.

It would be impossible not to mention the assistance received from Dave Parker for his valuable knowledge of layout and composition.

And, I could not close out this acknowledgement without a memtion to Viki Baudean who spends hours correcting my numerous grammar, spelling, punctuation and construction errors. It is a task which most writers cannot and will not attempt. It seems that once a writer has penned a line or a paragraph, he or she can read it over a hundred times never finding simple errors — because they see the words as they should be — correct. It takes an objective person with an excellent knowledge of basic English to correct a manuscript. And, thankfully, I have such a person to do this for me — else my attempts at writing would come to a halt.

Respectfully,

John E. Cayford

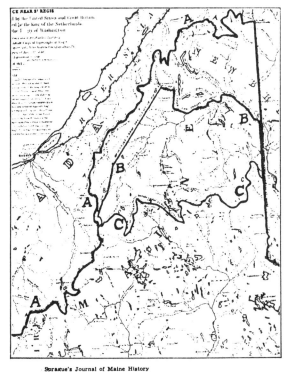

Sprague's Journal of Maine History

A NORTHEASTERN BOUNDARY MAP

Published March, 1843. Drawn from surveys made by authority of Congress.

Border dispute between England and US caused Fort Knox building. US claimed line A; British claimed line C; both settled on present line B after 60 years.

INTRODUCTION

I suspect many historians overlook obvious landmarks in their home state to seek out exciting events or people about which to research and write. I live less than twenty miles north of Fort Knox and have visited this fine fortification more than two hundred times in the past forty years. As a young grammar school boy, I played on the remparts, in the gun batteries, and even slid down the muzzle of the big 15 inch Rodman cannons. Years later, I returned to the fort using it as a base of operations for diving activities.

I had had reports of cannons being thrown into the river in front of the fort as well as a huge chain, its links large enough to allow a six foot person to stand inside, formerly stretched from the fort to the tip of Verona Island. After many diving hours in rough currents, these reports proved false.

During the 1960s, I returned to Fort Knox, once again using it as a base of operations in an effort to locate the charred remains of Colonial warships and transport vessels.

The ill-fated Penobscot Expedition, fought in Penobscot Bay, was America's largest naval defeat until the outbreak of World War II in 1941. This fleet of forty-five fine ships was destroyed or captured. The British salvaged almost one hundred cannons from this sunken fleet in 1779 immediately following the battle.

Ebenizah Clifford of New Hampshire came to Bangor in 1804 with his newly invented diving bell. Local inhabitants pointed out wreck sites and Mr. Clifford recovered about thirty cannons and several tons of cannon balls.

Bangor Harbor was dredged from 1870 to 1879 with about a dozen more cannons being recovered from the mud of the Penobscot River. It was not until the mid-1950s when work progressed on the Chamberlain Bridge project which spans the river from Bangor to Brewer did five more ship's cannons from Revolutionary vessels see the light of day.

This writer, also a professional diver, began researching the events of the ill-fated <u>Penobscot Expedition</u> hoping to recover more artifacts and possibly the remains of a vessel or two. It was late in 1957 when the first ship's hull was found and a Revere bronze 6-pounder cannon uncovered — a rare find as it is one of less than a dozen in the United States. As time would permit during the 1960s, I dove the river with Fort Knox serving as home base. Luck was with the diving crew as we discovered three more hulls.

The point is that during those numerous trips to and from Fort Knox, no thought was given to this magnificent fortification whatsoever. Thousands of people visited Fort Knox during those years and hundreds of thousands have been here since. I suspect they left the fort, like I did so many times, without really knowing the real story behind this great military garrison. I am certain that everyone marvels at the gigantic blocks of granite and the excellent masonary construction; shudder as they walk the narrow rifle galleries and move cautiously down the darkened passageways following the granite steps which lead deep beneath the ground. These same visitors are awed at the massive 15 inch Rodman cannon — the last survivor and solitary guardian of Fort Knox. However, none of us ever realized the monumental history behind this magnificent structure and the great engineering feats performed by the workmen.

Fort Knox is a casemated masonary fort built to defend the entrance of the Penobscot River when trouble erupted in the State of Maine's Aroostook County with the Province of New Brunswick over the United States border. Although the **Bloodless War** was settled before the construction of Fort Knox actually began, the government and the people of the Penobscot River Valley deemed it a necessary defensive measure.

Fort Knox served as a saging area and training camp for Maine soldiers during the Civil War. Connecticut troops trained and manned the garrison during the Spanish-American War. The Connecticut troops did not live inside the fort itself; they set up their tents and trained from them as they fully expected this would how they would live when shipped to Cuba and the War Zone.

The federal government spent nearly one million dollars in the building of Fort Knox. Yet, it was never totally completed. Minor sections of the garrison were left unfinished in 1869. Nevertheless, there is no doubt that Fort Knox is the most beautiful and the finest fortification of its kind in the Nation. This great monument is certainly a shining achievement to man's engineering and construction abilities. After visiting other fortifications in our country, one can only reflect back and know that Fort Knox is the best by far.

Personally, I am saddened that the federal government saw fit to sell the majority of the famed Rodman cannons for salvage or give them away. Not one flag remains that ever flew from the flagpole at Fort Knox. Today, this magnificent fortification belongs to the people of the State of Maine and is under the direction of the Maine Department of Conservation, who with their limited funds, have done an excellent job in preserving the site for nearly one hundred thousand people who visit the fort each year.

There are those visitors who think that our Fort Knox is the site where the United States keeps its gold reserve. They learn differently in a very short time. It would be nice if the Maine Department of Conservation had a pile of wooden ingots, painted gold, with wooden silhouettes of armed guards standing on either side of the ingot pile. Visitors could stand behind the ingot pile for picture taking. A sign to the side of the ingot pile would explain that these "gold" ingots are the only ones to be found at this Fort Knox.

It would also be nice if the gun carriages were replaced and cannons cast and placed on their empty mounts. The same applies to finishing the officers' and men's quarters. In the latter case, several rooms could be used for museum display purposes. Photos, drawings and paintings could line the walls depicting members of the Maine units stationed at the fort during the Civil War. The same would apply to the Connecticut men who served there. Staunch display cases could be made to contain military equipment, firearms, replicas of regimental and company flags, plus documents of all types.

Naturally to maintain a museum, personnel would be required to work in it. The State of Maine would employ young people during the summer months dressed in Civil War and Spanish-American War uniforms. They would perform a brief ceremony each hour on the parade grounds, fire their rifles and a small field cannon, and raise a regimental or company flag. During the remaining forty-five minutes of each hour, the "troops" would work as guides, in the museum, in a canteen, in a gift shop, as parking lot attendants or as grounds keepers.

As of recent date, portions of the fort have been closed due to weathering damage in some of the underground passages. The Fort Manager felt that for the safety of the visitors, it would be best to close off certain undergroung passages. The fort, being built at the bottom of a hill, gets all the run-off from rain and snow. Whereas the original drainage system is undoubtedly plugged, the run-off is seeping through the roof causing excessive damage below ground. This situation must be corrected in the very near future thereby preventing further damage. In these times of recession, it may prove well to be a benefit if the State of Maine considered a private non-profit corporation to take over the operation of Fort Knox.

Perhaps one day this will become a reality!!

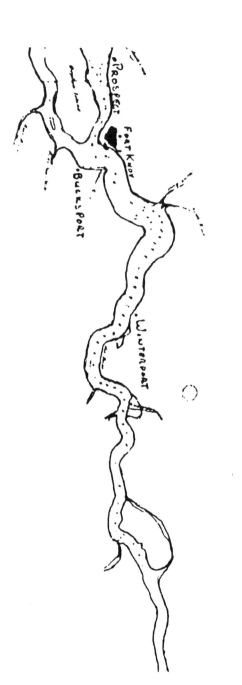

Early Penobscot River Map showing Fort Knox off the northwestern tip of Verona Island.

HISTORY OF PENOBSCOT BAY

The winding Penobscot River flows through the heart of the State of Maine. It is over 300 miles long with more than 1,600 streams and over 450 lakes pouring into its system. Named for the friendly Indian tribe who lived peacefully on its banks, the Penobscot had its own monumental history with the coming of the white man.

Penobscot Bay is the terminus of this great river. The eastern shore has been recognized as a strategic military center since 1605 when it was first extensively explored by Samuel de Champlain.

Castine — the Eden of the East — is located on the Majabagaduce peninsula. The French established a small garrison on the Pentagoet (Indian name) peninsula in 1635. It was commanded by a Major Biguyduce. It is supposed that the name Majabagaduce, with its numerous spellings, is attributed to that French officer. Castine is the only town in the United States to see the flags of four nations flying from the garrison flagpole. Whereas Castine was the most beautiful town on the entire Maine coast, it was the hub of activity in the Bay area.

The community received its present name from the original white settler and owner, French nobleman

Jean Vincent de St. Castine (1650 - 1722), whose marriage to Penobscot Indian Chief Madokawando's youngest daughter _Moon Witch_ so won him the Indian's regard, they considered him more than human.

The actual first recorded accounts of Penobscot Bay and the river began when Giovanni de Verrazano sailed into Penobscot Bay in 1524 for French King Francis I. Three years later, John Rut explored the interior of the State of Maine for England. Rasmusio's voyage in 1539 took him up the Penobscot River and he reported the fabled city of **Norumbega.** The most descriptive accounts of early Penobscot were written by Andre Trevet of France in 1556.

Explorers Simon Ferdinando (1576), Sir Humphrey Gilbert (1598), Bartholomew Gosnold (1602), Martin Pring and Eldred Jones (1603), Samuel de Champlain (1604), and Popham and Raleigh (1607) all made voyages into Penobscot Bay and up the river, telling of the great natural resources found while surveying the _Rhine of Maine_ for their own country's benefit.

Captain Hendrick Hudson claimed all of Penobscot Bay for Holland in 1609. Two years later, Father Biard of France selected a site for an Indian Mission at the junction of the Kenduskeag and Penobscot Rivers at Bangor.

The members of the Plymouth Colony established a trading post at Castine in 1628. Shortly thereafter, the French under d'Aulney began their encroachment of the Penobscot area in 1636. Father Leo of Paris built the first church in the Bay at Castine in 1648. The Dutch seafarer Captain Aeronouts captured Castine in 1674 flying the flag of Holland over the peninsula.

The 18th Century began with settlements dotting both sides of the Bay and river up to **The Falls** at Bangor. When the century was three-quarters past, the War for Independence began. It seemed far away for the residents of the District of Maine until the first naval engagement took place at Machias. This was followed by the shelling and burning of Falmouth (now Portland) and then in 1779, a British force captured Castine and controlled the entire area.

And American land and sea force was sent to Castine to dispell the British. However, their efforts were not very successful and nearly 40 fine ships were sunk in the river. The Penobscot River became a Revolutionary War graveyard. The only good purpose served by these sunken vessels was the many inhabitants along the river who lived off the items which they salvaged.

The War of 1812 caused concern in the Bay area. The British returned again and reestablished themselves at Castine, while capturing all the settlements up the Penobscot River as far as Bangor. When the war ended, the people in Penobscot Bay and all the river towns wanted protection from another

3

attack by any invader.

Bangor was becoming the commercial center of the area and the twin city of Brewer had six shipyards building the boats to transport Bangor's goods. This important industrial and commercial area had to be protected as well as the entrance to the Narrows of Penobscot River.

President Washington advised the Congress in 1793 to fortify the entire coastline of these new 13 colonies. Unfortunately, this advice went unheeded until 1795 when General Henry Knox presented a set of plans for harbor defense works which he drew up. General Knox had been Washington's Chief of Artillery and later the first Secretary of War in Washington's Cabinet. A small appropriation was voted by the congressional members for a survey and study.

The War of 1812 made it immediately clear to the Congress that adequate harbor defenses were a necessity. After the war, Congress moved and the construction of fortifications began in 1816. During the next 45 years, the majority of harbors on the East and Gulf Coasts were fortified with closed masonary forts. Only the State of Maine was forgotten in all this defensive construction; it was not until the clouds of war loomed again did the federal government recognize the necessity of fortifying the coast of Maine. Troubled with Great Britain over the border between the State of Maine and the Province of New Brunswick touched off the Aroostook (or Bloodless) War.

Public opinion was heard when the citizens from the Penobscot Bay town of Prospect drafted and passed a resolution dated May 25, 1840.

Resolution of Citizens of Prospect, Maine in favor of fortifying Penobscot Bay, May 25, 1840, referred to the Committee on Military Affairs.

Whereas, the Constitution of the United States imposes upon the General Government the obligation of protecting the lives and property of the citizens thereof from foreign invasion, and upon the citizens of the reciprocal duty of obedience and support. And whereas, this obligation extends to all important and national exigencies, as well as those of great and impending danger, as those of actual invasion; and whereas, the history of all nations, and especially that of our own country, has shown that a strong uniform, and permanent state of national defense is both the surest protection against the event of war, and the most human mode of mitigating its calamities; and whereas, the dilatory measures, hypocritical assurances, and war-like preparations, of Great Britain in relation to our northern boundry, but ill comport with the idea of an amicable adjustment of this "vexed question"; And whereas, the valley of the Penobscot River, embracing a territory of several hundred miles in extent, and a population of about 200,000, though capable of

5

being put in a state of defense at a trifling expense, and naturally exposed to and likely to receive the first attacks of a foreign foe, is utterly defenseless: Therefore, Resolved, unanimously, That, which we hold ourselves in readiness at all times to sustain the integrity of our State and the honor of the Union at the expense of our property and lives if need be, we call upon the General Government to afford us that protection against foreign invasion which the Constitution contemplates and enjoins.

Resolved, that the delay of Great Britain in effecting a settlement of the northeast boundry question, is but another development for the policy that has governed the British cabinet for centuries. To wit: First to make every treaty as indefinite as possible; then to set up a claim to territory, from the ambiguity or uncertainty of the treaty; then to negotiate upon the subject for the longest possible period; and, finally, to throw the sword into the balance, and dictate right by might.

Resolved, that it is the duty of Congress forthwith to make an appropriation to be immediately applied in fortifying the Penobscot River and bay.

Resolved, that should the prospect of war with Great Britain prove falacious, the duty of Congress to put the country in the state of defense will still be obligatory, and out to be discharged.

Resolved, that should war come in the present unprepared state of the country, the blood of our defenseless citizens will be upon the authors of that miserable economy that will have invited foreign insolence and aggression.

Voted, that the above resolutions should be signed by the chairman and secretary, and copies forwarded to our Representatives and Senators in Congress assembled, and also published in the Belfast Journal.

Joseph Ames, Chairman

Timo. B. Grant, Secretary

The Congress voted to spend $25,000 for the construction of a fort at or near the junction of the Mattawamkeag and Penobscot Rivers on September 9, 1841. Property was never purchased nor work commenced at this site.

Major-General Henry Knox, Soldier and Statesman, 1st.
Secretary of War in President Washington's Cabinet, and
the man for whom Fort Knox and Knox County was named.

MAJOR-GENERAL HENRY KNOX

The fort located at the Narrows of Penobscot River was officially named for Major-General Henry Knox of Boston, Massachusetts, and Thomaston, Maine, on January 31, 1849. The federal government could have selected no finer man after which to name the fortification that would stand as proudly as did the man himself.

Henry Knox, Major-General, Continental Army, and the first Secretary of War in President Washington's Cabinet, was the man for whom any number of forts then under construction could have been named. His father William, of Scotch-Irish descent, and his Irish mother, Mary Campbell, came to the Colonies in 1729, landing at Boston. They married in February, 1735, and in the ensuing years, had ten children. Henry was son number seven. Mr. Knox was a ship master, but suffered financial reverses. He died in the West Indies at age fifty.

Young Henry was only ten years old when his father passed away and this immediately placed him in the position of being his mother's sole support. He left grammar school and found employment in the bookstore of Wharton and Bowes, Boston.

Henry spent his idle hours reading all the books on military subjects to be found on the shelves. On his 21st birthday, Henry Knox opened his own bookstore. *The London Book-Store* was a haven for British officers and their trade brought him a fair income. His mother died a few months after the store's opening on December 14, 1771. The shop remained in business until 1774.

Henry enlisted in a local militia company when he was only eighteen. On March 4, 1770, at the scene of the infamous **Boston Massacre,** he endeavored to keep British Captain Preston from firing into the gathered crowd. Later, while on a hunting trip, he lost the third and fourth fingers on his left hand when his rifle exploded.

Young Henry joined the elite *Boston Grenadier Corps* in 1772. He was second-in-command under Captain Joseph Pierce. He made a full study of military science and engineering. Knox possessed a martial bearing which attracted the attention of Lucy Flucker, daughter of the Royal Secretary of the Province, Thomas Flucker. The couple was married on June 16, 1774, against her family's wishes.

When the Revolutionary started, Knox and his wife left Boston in June, 1775. He presented himself to General Artemus Ward as a volunteer. From that time on, his career in the military was extremely active and he participated in nearly every major campaign of the war. His achievements and promotions in the military read like a fairy tale. His experience as an artillery expert was graciously accepted by the Colonists. He became one of General Washington's closest friends and advisors.

General Washington commissioned Knox as a colonel on November 17, 1775, and placed him in charge of artillery for the Continental Army. He suggested to General Washington that driving the British from Boston would require more artillery which could be obtained from Fort Ticonderoga in New York. Ethan Allen and his Green Mountain Men had captured the British fort and all the ordnance on May 10. Washington approved the plan, so Knox and his brother William dragged a train of artillery from New York, arriving at Boston in late January, 1776. This act strengthened his reputation for resourcefulness and daring. He positioned his guns at Dorchester Heights and the fire power forced General Howe's British regulars to evacuate Boston with Colonel Knox's in-laws and 1,100 other Loyalists.

Henry reported to General Washington at Long Island, New York after laying out defenses in Rhode Island and Connecticut. He took part in battles around New York. It was Colonel Henry Knox who directed Washington's troops when they crossed the ice-jammed Delaware River on Christmas eve, 1776, and capturing over 1,200 Hessian troops. Washington thanked Colonel Knox for his service in public orders and promoted him to the rank of Brigadier-General.

During the fall campaign of 1777, General Knox's Regiment fought with their usual intrepidity at

Brandywine and Germantown. The following year, his artillery reduced the British at the Battle of Monmouth on June 28, 1778.

It is to the credit of General Henry Knox, who, in 1779, made the first move for the establishment of a military academy, which later became **West Point.** He was one of the court-martial officers who tried Major John Andre, the British spy in 1780. General Washington declared that *the resources of his genius supplied the deficit of means* when he referred to Knox's placement of the American artillery at the Siege of Yorktown in 1781. Shortly after the surrender of General Lord Cornwallis at Yorktown, Henry Knox was commissioned a Major–General on November 15, 1781.

Following the close of hostilities, General Knox was stationed at **West Point,** and in August, 1782, was given command of that post. A year later, the ragtail army of George Washington was disbanded. The General said farewell to his staff in December. Knox resigned from the military in January, 1784, going home to Boston, where he was appointed by the Massachusetts General Court with a commission to treat with the Penobscot Indians.

Knox accepted the election mandate by the Federal Congress as the Secretary of War on March 8, 1785. In January, 1787, he sent General Washington a rough sketch for a general government. As a staunch supporter of the new Constitution, Knox was retained

as the Secretary of War when the President's Cabinc
was formed.

When Knox tallied the standing army, he found
only 700 men. He submitted a comprehensive plan
in 1790 for a national militia, but it was rejected
by Congress. Alexander Hamilton, the Secretary
of the Treasury, had a conflict with Knox about which
department of the President's Cabinet should purchase
military supplies and stores. Henry promoted the
negotations of treaties with the Indians and tried
to persuade Congress for both an adequate navy and
coastal fortifications. Henry Knox retired to private
life on December 28, 1794.

The General and Mrs. Knox settled in their imposing
mansion *Montpelier* in June, 1796. It was built on
the vast estate inherited by Mrs. Knox from her
maternal grandfather, General Samuel Waldo. Both
General Knox and General Waldo have counties in
the State of Maine named after them.

Knox's great home was located near Thomaston
at the head of the St. Georges River. Here, he engaged
in brickmaking, lumbering, ship building and cattle
raising. He built the first water canal, complete
with lock gates, in the United States. He also spent
great sums of money and entertained lavishly.
Montpelier was host to many distinguished foreigners
including Alexander Baring, Talleyrand, and Louis
Philippe.

Misfortune befell the Knox family as nine of their twelve children died very young, only three surviving their parents.

The General died most unexpectedly when a chicken bone lodged in his intestines. His death occurred on October 25, 1806, at the age of fifty-six. The General was buried at Thomaston with full military honors. A shaft of limestone marks his gravesite. Mrs. Knox died in 1824.

It is for this illustrious American that the fortification at the Narrows of Penobscot River in Prospect, Maine was named. The federal government could have made no finer choice.

Adjutant-General Jones in Washington, D.C., issued General Order No. 6 on January 31, 1849.

The following military works in process of construction, will hereinafter be known by the names set opposite them, which have been approved by the Secretary of War.

The fort at the Narrows of the Penobscot River, Maine --- FORT KNOX.

CONSTRUCTING THE FORT

It was 1840 when the townsfolk of Prospect, Maine sent their resolution to the members of the United States Congress. The northeastern boundry between the State of Maine and British Canada's New Brunswick Province had not been settled and the bay area citizens were worried as to what Great Britain might do next. It had only been about twenty-five years since the British had occupied and devastated the countryside. They were very likely to return, a prospect which the Penobscot Bay citizenry did not look forward to with any excitement.

Congress moved and voted an appropriation of $25,000 on September 9, 1841, under Chapter 17. A fortification was to be built some thirty miles north of Bangor at the junction of the Mattawamkeag and Penobscot Rivers. For reasons not mentioned in Congressional or military correspondence, a permanent site was never selected nor did any construction commence. Pressure was brought to bear on the Nation's lawmakers in the Capitol, and two years later they moved again.

The Twenty-Seventh Congress during the 3rd Session, under STATUTES AT LARGE, V, dated March 3, 1843, passed an appropriation in Section 2, Chapter 2 of the Congressional Records.

Be it enacted by the Senate and House of

Representatives of the United States of America in Congress assembled, That the following sums be, and they are hereby appropriated, to be paid out of any unappropriated money in the Treasury, for the preservation, repair, and construction of certain fortifications, for the half calender year beginning on the first day of January and ending on the thirtieth day of June, one thousand eight hundred and forty-three: and for the fiscal year beginning on the first day of July, one thousand eight hundred and forty-three, and ending on the thirtieth day of June, one thousand eight hundred and forth-four:

And be it further enacted, That the sum of twenty-five thousand dollars, appropriated by the act of Congress, approved ninth of September, one thousand eight hundred and forty-one, for defensive works, barracks, and other necessary buildings, and purchase of a site for a depot at or near the junction of the Mattawamkeag and Penobscot Rivers, Maine, may be applied to the purchase of a site and commencement of defensive works at or near the Narrows of the Penobscot River, Maine.

Immediate steps were taken to obtain the high ground opposite the town of Bucksport on the west bank of the Penobscot River in Waldo County. What historical significance this land had! It was formerly owned by General Samuel Waldo, a hero in his own right, and the very ground selected by General Peleg Wadsworth and Colonel Paul Revere in 1779 where the American forces would establish a defensive work should a retreat be necessary for the troops of the Penobscot Expedition. The Expedition went into a retreat. However, the site was never occupied by the Colonials as mass confusion prevented this action.

The section obtained by the United States Government looked like two section pieces of pie. John Pierce and William French owned the largest tracts with smaller acreage being purchased from Hannah R. Harriman, Daniel H. Harriman, and John Lee. The deeds were purchased between September 4, 1843 and March 23, 1844, and are recorded in volumes 46 and 50 respectively in the Deed Records of Waldo County.

The government had obtained approximately one hundred and twenty-five acres on which to build their fort. About ninety acres of the purchase was woodlands. The countryside in the immediate vicinity of the proposed fort was mountainous with a second growth of light timber consisting principally of hemlock, pine, birch and beech. The soil was a brownish clay mixture. The average temperature was 55°F., and the climate was considered cold. The exact site of the fortification is latitude 44:33'58" and longitude 68:48'08". The land was purchased for the sum of $6,510.00, and the sale and transfer was finalized by U.S. Land Agent J. C. Loomis on March 23, 1844.

The government ordered Brevet Major Isaac I. Stevens, an engineer of the Coast Survey Office, to make a complete survey of the land and to lay

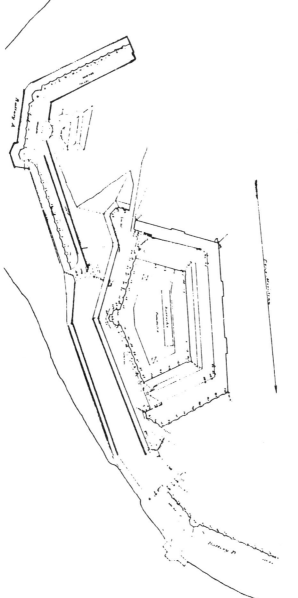

Original Plans of Fort Knox after outlying gun batteries had been constructed.

Fort Knox

Office of the Chief of Engineers, Feb 1866.

out the original fort, then designated only as the *Fort at the Narrows in Penobscot River.* The natural contour of the land provided Major Stevens with a design for a fortification that was predominantly underground.

The fort was in the shape of a pentagon (five sided), with the front walls facing the river. Only the gun implacements, located on the right and left parapets and to the rear of the fort on the terreplein, would be in the open. The largest artillery pieces would be protected by the fort's mighty walls. To the rear of the fort was high ground which offered protection as well as an observation post.

Two miles west of the fort was located Mount Waldo in the town of Frankfort. The mountain is approximately one thousand feet high and composed entirely of granite, lying in sheets of varying thickness, constituting the most remarkable granite quarry in New England, if not the entire United States. This granite would be quarried and would serve to build the finest casemated fort in the Nation.

Excavation commenced late in July, 1844, and proceeded without interruption during the remainder of the working year. In 1845 and 1846, a full force of men was employed to prepare the ground for granite which would be forthcoming.

Only a small work force was employed for about two months in 1848. Yet, the amount of work executed from October 1st was outstanding. More than fifteen thousand yards of stone was excavated, plus ten thousand yards of earth, the majority of which was used to build a roadway, the north and west glacis, and the parade grounds.

Six months of labor was performed in 1849 with a full force of one hundred and eleven men, which included an assistant overseer, 1 clerk, 1 fort keeper, 1 sub-overseer, 2 bargemen, 3 smiths (blacksmiths), 2 carpenters, 9 teamsters, 35 quarrymen, and 55 laborers. The main work force was applied to excavating stone from the work site. All the earth covering the stone excavation of the parade grounds and ditches of the main project was removed and placed in the north and west glacis. The embankment of earth involved in the extension of Gun Battery A and the roadway from the wharf was finished. The engineer-in-charge requested an appropriation from the Congress of $75,000 for the ensuing fiscal year.

Major Stevens planned on finishing the general project by 1856, based on six annual appropriations: five in the amount of $75,000 each, and one for $65,000. His projected work schedule was very detailed.

In 1850, the workers would complete the blasting and raise the north extremity of enrockment by eleven thousand yards. Casemated traverse batteries A and B, plus the sustaining wall, would be near completion before the cold weather stopped the work.

The following year, three hot shot furnaces would be constructed for A and B batteries as both these gun batteries would be finished. The scarp would be raised to the full height on the north and water fronts. A sod cover face would be placed to the level of the roadway, and foundations and piers for the casemates and posterns built.

The scarp would be raised to full height in 1852, plus the foundations and piers for the remaining casemates, arches, backing, posterns, and the parade grounds' wall would be complete. At this time, the quarrymen, master stone cutter and teamsters would be transporting the huge granite blocks from Mount Waldo.

Work was progressing as a wharf of sixty feet head and approximately ninety-five feet in length was constructed of the stone quarried out from the ledge on the fort side. There was an addition connected to the main wharf by a wing fifty feet long. The walls surrounding this wing are of granite and corresponds with the masonry of the main wharf. Running in the rear of the ledge stone wharf, a granite wall, one hundred and twenty feet in length, was constructed, sustaining the roadway from the wharf to Gun Battery A. The sustaining wall on the inner side of the road and in front of Gun Battery B was extended. Considerable work was done in the vicinity of the walls to provide for an efficient drainage to Battery B and its traverse.

Return of Officers and Hired Men at Fort
Knox for the month of November – 1864 –

Officers

Present	Absent
	Major. Thos Lincoln Casey Corps of Engineers P.O. Address, Portland, Maine.

Hired Men

Number	Trade or Occupation	Time or piece Work	Wages	Amount	
1	Gen'l Overseer	30	days	4.00	120	00
1	Overseer	30	"	3.00	90	00
1	Clerk	1 Month		55.00	55	00
1	Draughtsman	26	days	2.75	71	50
1	Clerk	24	"	1.75	42	00
1	Sub Overseer	26	"	2.00	52	00
1	Master Carpenter	15.1	"	2.75	42	90
2	Carpenters	44	"	2.65	116	60
1	"	16.4	"	2.40	39	36
1	"	2.9	"	1.75	5	07
2	Engineers	47.4	"	2.40	113	72
3	Blacksmiths	65.3	"	2.75	179	57
1	"	23.4	"	2.60	60	14

Return of Officers and Hired Men during the
month of November, 1864. Document shows
the daily and monthly wages paid each trade.

During 1854, the rampart of the main fort was to be completed along with the construction of thirty gun platforms. Paving, sidewalks, privies, cisterns, drainage works and sodding and earth embanking was scheduled.

The following year would see many individual projects completed. Quarters, sodding, grading, surface drainage, cover face, parade field, and Battery C would be finished also.

Only the men's barracks remained to be completed during 1856. The original fort would have been constructed for the sum of $475,000 according to Major Stevens' plans. However, like most military construction projects, this did not transpire.

The beautiful granite from Mount Waldo began flowing into the work site in 1851. The Mount Waldo Granite Company began operations under the direction of George A. Pierce and John P. Rowe. Dynamite and black powder was used to obtain the slabs. The greatest difficulty was in transporting the granite blocks to the work site. Rails were laid down and railway *mules* were used to guide the blocks down the mountain. Then, they were attached to galamanders and drawn by oxen and/or teams of horses to barges waiting in the river.

The master stone cutter and his assistants were responsible for producing the blocks of equal thickness and length, while the teamsters, bargemen and laborers brought in the stone and performed the non-skilled work.

Stone cutters and quarrymen were not plentiful in the State of Maine and the government went overseas to England and Ireland to obtain the necessary professionals to work the fine granite at Mount Waldo. After the fort was erected, many of the quarrymen and stone cutters stayed in the State of Maine which was the beginning of the great Irish families in our state.

Once the great blocks of granite were in place at the fort, the master mason and his assistants took over from this point.

The following is a list of the officers-in-charge of the construction at Fort Knox:

(The official military rank for these officers is given; not the breveted or honorary rank they often carried.)

Lieut. Isaac I. Stevens,
July, 1844 — Dec., 1847

Lt.-Col. Sylvanus Thayer,
Dec.,1847 — Dec.,1849

Capt. Isaac I. Stevens,
Jan.,1850 — March,1853

Major John L. Smith,
April,1853 — Sept.,1854

Capt. William S. Frazer,
Oct.,1854 — Dec.,1855

Lieut. John D. Kurtz,
April,1856 — March,1861

Capt. Thomas L. Casey,
Aug.,1861 — June,1865

(Unable to determine)
Dec.,1865 — July,1866

Capt. Godfrey Weitzel,
July,1866 — May,1867

Major Thomas L. Casey,
June,1867 — Nov.,1867

Lt.-Col. George Thom,
Nov.,1867 — June,1868

Lt.-Col. James C. Duane,
Aug.,1868 — May,1879

Lt.-Col. Charles E. Blunt,
May,1879 — 1866

Lt.-Col. Jared A. Smith,
1886 — 1891

Lt.-Col. Peter C. Haines,
1892

Construction at Fort Knox did not cease by **1856** as proposed in the schedule of Engineer Isaac **Stevens.** Additional gun emplacements were built **and further** improvements expanded the orginal design. The work on the major portion of the fort terminated in 1869 with only the interior of the men's quarters left unfinished. A total of $928,500 had been appropriated by the Congress and spent in building this magnificent fortification. Inside the main fort, the most outstanding piece of craftsmanship is the spiral staircase; there is one located at each end of the parade grounds. The spiral staircase is built of solid pieces of granite in a complete circular column formed by the treads and risers. It is a masterpiece of the stone cutters' and engineers' craftsmanship and abilities.

The long shooting galleries, which surround the dry moat on the sides and to the rear of the fort, were designed to protect the installation from any land attack. The longest gallery is the one located to the rear of the fort next to the men's quarters. This gallery is approximately five feet wide and over three hundred feet long, situated on different elevations. These narrow shooting galleries were restricted for rifle fire only.

The large gun galleries were placed on the two frontal facades of the pentagonal shaped fort. These galleries were for the eight inch and ten inch cannons which were mounted on semicircular pintles nearly ten feet in diameter. The pintles acted as rails thereby allowing the guns to be swung in any desired direction, throwing shot clear across the Penobscot River. The cannons were protected by large, massive granite walls over one and a half feet thick. The firepower of the numerous gun batteries was awesome.

The parade ground is located in the center of the fort's pentagonal design. The grounds were used to drill the troops and to hold weekly inspections. The flagpole stood on the parade grounds flying flags containing as few as twenty-seven stars and up to fifty. Unfortunately, there is not a single flag remaining today which flew from the summit of the Fort Knox flagpole.

The men's quarters were built of brick and granite and they were bombproof. The walls were approximately three feet thick and the floors were dirt. The eight compartments, measuring thirty by fifteen feet each, were heated by a main furnace located in the first compartment. (It must have been rather chilly for those men quartered in the last few compartments!!)

A report dated 1869 from Major Thomas Lincoln Casey, the engineer-in-charge, stated that during the past year, the north covered way, northeast drive-bastion and defensive gallery, together with the closure wall and caponniers of the north ditch had been completed. The south and west glacis were brought to grade for a distance of some fifty feet from their crests. Some progress was made with the storerooms, in the parade grounds of the main works, and a large amount of the finish of the quarters in the west front was put in. Two fifteen inch cannon platforms were completed in Batteries A and B, and seven platforms for front pintle guns in the north covered way.

During this present year, it was proposed to complete the storerooms of the parade grounds area, except for their mastic coverings, the banquettes of the north counter scarp gallery, the magazine of the northeast demibastion, plus nine positions for guns requiring only their traverse irons. The postern doors of the main fort as well as the outworks will also be hung.

The engineer asked for an appropriation of $50,000 for the next fiscal year.

A description of Fort Knox by the Ordnance Sergeant in charge as Fort Keeper outlines the construction of the fortification in 1870:

QUARTERS: The officers' quarters in the main works are unfinished and built of brick and granite — bombproof. They are divided into two seperate buildings, two rooms to each building; each room measures fifty by twenty feet, containing five small rooms which are temporary.

The men's quarters in the main works are unfinished and built of brick and granite — bombproof. They are divided into eight compartments, each one measuring about thirty by fifteen feet, and now used as magazines. There is also one building used for men's quarters outside the main works, wood frame construction, measuring one hundred by twenty feet, which is temporary.

STOREHOUSES: There are two storehouses inside the main works, one of which is used for implements appertaining to the ordnance at the post. The buildings measure fifty by fifteen feet with a capacity of six thousand seven hundred and fifty cubic feet. Their condition is leaky. The storehouses are bombproof and built of brick and granite.

HOSPITAL, GUARDROOM, etc.: There are nine old wood frame buildings occupied at present by the Engineer Department as a blacksmith shop, carpenter shop, implement houses and office. There is one large barn, seventy-five by twenty-five feet, in good condition. There is also one unfinished wood frame building intended for a kitchen, but now stored with wood belonging to the Quartermaster's Department.

FUEL, FORAGE and WATER: Fuel is delivered to the fort and obtained by local purchase. Forage is obtained by purchase at the post also. There are two springs of water in the main works, besides several cisterns.

COMMUNICATIONS: Between the fort and the nearest town is a steam ferry boat.

COMPOUND: There was at one time an animal compound maintained at the fort for the post animals.

It appears from this 1870 report that no work, or at best, very little work was being done at Fort

Knox. Appropriations do not show that any major construction was undertaken after 1869. The records do show that small sums were taken from petty cash accounts to make repairs to buildings when they were on the verge of falling into total disrepair.

Captain Thomas Ward from the Office of the Inspector General, Department of the East, made an inspection of the ungarrisoned post of Fort Knox, Maine, on November 17, 1883. Captain Ward stated that storm doors and windows on the north side of the house occupied by the Ordnance Sergeant were necessary and that the roof on the south side needed reshingling; new floors and general repairs were also needed at a probable cost not to exceed two hundred dollars.

He further stated that the roof inside the fort used as the Ordnance Storeroom leaked and required attention.

Upon reference, the Chief Quartermaster of the Department recommended that authority be granted for repairing the storeroom, provided funds could be supplied to the Quartermaster General in addition to the allotment made to that Department.

Major-General Hancock approved the above recommendation at a cost of two hundred dollars, and the Quartermaster General recommended that the two hundred dollars be authorized from the *Barracks and Quarters Reserve Fund* for making the necessary repairs.

Future construction was planned at Fort Knox as late as 1900, and the necessary funding was approved by the Congress to construct a torpedo storehouse. It was built from brick and was to house buoyant torpedoes (submarine mines) which would be placed in the river in the event of another attack or war. From this point on, Fort Knox fell into a state of disrepair.

Spiral Staircase. Solid granite slabs coming to a circular colume is a masterpiece of engineering.

Parade Grounds. Officer's Quarters at the far end;
gun batteries in casemates to the left.

Rodman 15 inch Cannons -- the most powerful guns
at Fort Knox,

ORDNANCE and EXPLOSIVES

Heavy artillery was of two types prior to and
during the Civil War: (1). the siege gun, and (2).
the sea coast gun of the Rodman principle.

The Rodman gun (cannon) was the primary defensive
weapon at Fort Knox. The gun, while having to some
extent its peculiarity of form, was principally
distinguished by the mode adopted in its manufacture,
which was an invention of Major T. J. Rodman, U.
S. Army.

33

The casting was made around a hollow core, or core-barrel as it was specifically termed, into which was introduced a stream of cold water, the outside of the casting being kept heated until the cooling from the interior reached the outer portion of the mass of metal forming the casting. It was claimed that this mode of manufacture insured two important advantages over the old method of casting the gun solid and then boring it out. The strain upon the metal by cooling in large masses was reversed, rendering the gun less liable to burst from the explosion of the powder in it; and a much greater degree of hardness was given to the interior surface rendering the gun less liable to abrasion in the bore by the passage of the projectile along it, and the action of the gases of the powder upon the metal. It was generally held by the witnesses that no effective gun of large caliber could be made of cast iron except upon the Rodman principle, or the principle of cooling from the interior.

Batteries A and B at Fort Knox had the famed fifteen inch Rodman guns. These weapons weighed twenty-five tons and were the largest cannons used in the defense of the Nation's Capitol during the Civil War.

The Rodman fifteen inch cannon was first made in 1860, and was the most powerful weapon then known. Rodman guns were smoothbore; they did not have riflings which caused the projectile to rotate in a spiral motion thereby allowing it to travel a greater distance.

Gunpowder was the prime explosive employed by the military. Gunpowder was composed of seventy-five parts of nitre, fifteen parts of charcoal, and ten parts of sulphur. It was glazed to enable it to resist exposure to moisture and the effects of shaking while in transit.

This mixture of gunpowder burned at a temperature between five hundred and seventy-five (575°) and six hundred (600?) degrees Fahrenheit. If the gunpowder was made of pure materials, well glazed, and kept in proper casks stored in a dry magazine, it absorbed less than one percent of moisture in ten to fifteen years. If the gunpowder was left freely exposed to air saturated with moisture, it would absorb two percent and more moisture in a twenty-four period.

There have been numerous types of projectiles introduced for cannon fire from round solid balls to simple nuts and bolts. The most common type of projectile was the solid shot.

The **Solid Shot** was spherical and its weight in pounds was used to designate the caliber of the gun to which it belonged. For example, early cannons were referred to as 6-pounders or 12-pounders, etc., which meant that the projectile it fired weighed approximately that much.

These cannon balls were cast and their composition included graphite. Many cannon balls found in sea water after years of submersion weigh only ounces. The electrolysis action which takes place in sea water removes the iron depositing it elsewhere, leaving only the graphite in its original shape. Six pound solid shot recently recovered from Revolutionary War wrecks in the Penobscot River had the shape and size, but weighed less than one pound.

The **Shell** was a hollow shot, with such thickness of metal as enabled it to penetrate earth works, wooden buildings, and wooden vessels without breaking. It was charged with powder just prior to being placed into the cannon. Shells burst with great force spreading jagged pieces of metal in a wide area, such as the fragmentation hand grenade of World War II.

Fire was introduced to the explosive charge by means of a fuse inserted into the hole through which the powder was introduced. The time of the explosion was regulated by the preparation of the fuse. Shells were intended to burst inside the object at which they were aimed. Shells used in long range fire were found to be less accurate than solid shot. The shell was also designated by the weight of solid shot of the same diameter.

Canister shot consisted of a tin cylinder, attached to a sabot and filled with cast iron shot, much like buck shot. These shots varied in diameter and in weight depending upon the caliber and cannon in which they were used. Canister shots were packed in sawdust four tiers high. The lower tier rested on a rolled iron plate, which was placed on the sabot. Then, the canister was closed with a sheet iron cover.

Hot Shot was the term describing solid cannon balls which had been heated prior to firing. Hot shot was used to set a ship's hull and/or rigging on fire. Hot shot furnaces were erected at sea coast fortifications.

The hot shot furnace at Fort Knox is located near the waterfront in the southeast quadrant. The small brick building measures approximately five by ten feet. Coal was fed into the furnace through two or three doors located near the base. Two round holes are found in each end of the building approximately three-quarters up from the base. These holes are connected by iron bars upon which the cannon balls were placed. This furnace held sixty or more shot depending upon the size.

The shot being placed and the furnace being cold, it required one hour and fifteen minutes to heat them to a red color. After the furnace was heated, a twenty-four pound shot could be brought to a red heat in less than thirty minutes. It required the services of three men to attend the furnace.

The hot shot furnace required the following implements: 2 pokers made from three-quarter inch round iron stock, five and a half feet long, with the end bent to a right angle. These were used to stir the fire; 2 iron forks, made from the same round iron stock, were employed to remove the shot from the furnace. These forks had to be dipped in water to cool them after every other ball was removed from the furnace. A large metal rasp (file) was used to remove scales from the balls should they become overheated.

A pair of tongs with circular jaws was used for taking up the shot and an iron rake was used to remove the cinders from the ashpit. A trough or tub, a bucket, a barrel, and a rammer with the head covered by a circular plate of sheet iron slightly larger in diameter than the cannon ball, which was used to remove clay that could stick to the insides of the cannon barrel when clay wads were employed.

A metal ladle for carrying the hot shot balls from the furnace to the cannon completed the necessary tool inventory. The ladle was formed of an iron ring with its interior bevelled to fit the size ball being transported. The ladle was two arms which were fitted with wooden handles.

Wadding was used to pack the cannon balls and explosive charge in the cannon barrel. These waddings were necessary to make the cannon discharge whereas explosive gases seek the easiest route from confinement to natural atmosphere. In the case of black powder rifles, if wadding was not employed, both the powder and shot would fall out of the barrel if the gun were pointed in a direction whereby the tip of the barrel was lower than the stock. The wadding also served to contain the explosive gases thus enabling the charge to "blast" the shot out of the barrel and over a distance. The greater the amount of powder used, the further the shot would travel — provided the rifleman or the cannonier did not use too much powder which would cause his barrel to explode.

Wads were generally made from dry hay pressed and packed firmly in the cannon barrel by the rammer. Wads employed when firing hot shot were made from good clay, which was abundant along the banks of the Penobscot River. The clay had to be free from sand and/or gravel, and moistened just enough to work well. The wads were cylindrical and one caliber long. When good clay was not available, it was preferable to use hay wads that had been soaked in water for fifteen minutes. They were removed from the water and allowed to drip until the remaining liquid was absorbed by the hay. This use of the moisture wadding kept the heat from the hot shot from prematurely igniting the powder causing a serious accident.

Cartridge was the term applied to the explosive charge packed into a cannon barrel. Cartridges for hot shot were made from cannon cartridge paper — a parchment well pasted to prevent the powder from shifting or spilling out. Hot shot cartridges were always carefully examined before they were used to ascertain that no holes had been accidently punched in them. The use of two cartridge bags, one within the other, was a deterrent to punctures.

Loading hot shot was different than loading cold balls. The cartridge was rammed into the cannon followed by a wad of dry hay carefully rammed. The cannon muzzle was elevated sufficiently to allow the shot ball to roll in. A wet hay wad or clay wad was pressed into the barrel and a second clay wad, only half a caliber long followed. This completed the loading procedure.

It was a standard practice and a good precaution to pass a wet sponge into the cannon barrel prior to putting in the shot. When wet hay wads were used, steam issued from the touchhole (firing vent) as soon as the ball was in place. This action was caused by the effect of the heat of the hot shot upon the water contained in the wads. No danger resulted from this action as the ball was allowed to cool within the cannon barrel without the explosive charge catching fire. However, it was better to fire the cannon without too much delay as excessive steam could render the powder useless.

The penetration of both cold and hot shot into wood was equal under the same conditions and same circumstances. Yet, a fire was communicated more rapidly in the wood of a structure or ship's hull when the ball would not penetrate more than ten to twelve inches. If the ball penetrated deeper, the external air was not sufficiently free around hot shot to cause ignition of the wood. Therefore, it was proper to fire hot shot with small charges, one-quarter to one-sixth the weight of the shot being discharged.

The weight of the charge was determined according to the distance of the object being fired at and so that the shot would remain in the wooden structure and not penetrate too deeply. A red-hot cannon ball would retain sufficient heat to set fire to a ship's wooden hull after striking the water several times. Heated shot did not return to its original dimensions on cooling, but retained a permanent enlargement.

One must marvel at the expertise of the gunners in those early days. The gun powder mixtures were not consistant in either mixture or care and handling. One batch could be moisture free while the next could be almost useless. The master gunner knew his material by feel and smell. And most remarkable was the ability to aim the cannon and fire it on a rolling and pitching vessel. If the shot was fired when the ship was pitching all the shots would end up in the water alongside the vessel. If the shots were fired when the ship was rolling, the shots would go into the air and their range would either be too short or pass over the other target harmlessly. Gunners in fortifications firing at approaching ships had to judge the speed of the vessel, its distance, and load the cannon with the correct amount of powder to reach the vessel, have the cannon ball pierce the hull, and cause as much damage as possible. These were remarkable feats accomplished with very primitive weapons.

Empty Gun Emplacements of Battery A looking north at Fort.

ORDNANCE REPORTS

There were one hundred and eleven pieces of heavy artillery at Fort Knox in June, 1864, all of which were shipped off to the fighting area.

In November that same year, twenty-seven pieces of field artillery were at the post, but no heavy cannons.

In December, 1865, the garrison reported fifty-seven pieces of heavy artillery and twelve pieces of mountain artillery.

After fifteen years of inactivity — with regards to troops in station — the Board of Army Engineers inspected all military fortifications and made recommendations as to which forts could be placed on the inactive list. Their report, dated November 30, 1881, states:

Commencing with the Coast of Maine,
the first order is:

FORT KNOX

Situated upon the Penobscot River, opposite Bucksport, at the Narrows, 18 miles below Bangor.

This structure is essentially finished in accordance with its original plans. It is a casemated work of excellent masonry. Its exterior barbette batteries, however, are mainly relied upon for the defense of this position against a hostile fleet. These batteries are mostly prepared for ten inch smoothbore guns. Modified to receive the most improved models of the recent, nine, ten, and twelve inch rifled guns, with the aid of torpedoes, they will resist effectually the passage of a hostile squadron, and thus secure the anchorage above for our own vessels that may take refuge there and to protect Bangor.

This fort should be retained and put in condition to accomplish the purpose of its construction as above set forth, but since nine inch rifled guns and a few fifteen inch guns can be mounted in its batteries as they now exist, there is no immediate demand for this immediate modification.

Colonel R. P. Hughes, The Inspector General from Headquarters, Department of the East, Washington, D.C., reported from Bucksport on August 30, 1897, that the armament of Fort Knox consisted of:

25 ten inch Rodman guns mounted enbarbette on front pintle carriages.

3 fifteen inch Rodman guns mounted enbarbette on center pintle carriages.

14 ten inch Rodman guns mounted in casemates on front pintle carriages.

12 twenty-four pound flank defense guns on wooden carriages.

There were also:

5 eight inch casemate carriages on emplacements without guns, and,

14 ten inch barbette front pintle carriages in position without guns.

There were on hand:

2,100 ten inch shot

2,800 ten inch shells, and,

300 fifteen inch shells.

As these carriages, from which the guns have been taken, give the work a very unmilitary appearance, and the situation is visible to travellers on the river, I have instructed the sergeant to submit <u>Inventory and Inspection Reports</u> on which formal recommendations will be made.

Unfortunately, after the Spanish-American War, the government saw fit to give away many of the guns of Fort Knox. They were given to cities, towns, and organizations to decorate soldiers' monuments, statues, cemetery memorials, and town squares. The remaining heavy artillery was sold by the Salvage Officer at Portland Harbor.

Mr. Thomas Burke of Boston, Massachusetts, was

the successful bidder on the weapons and other salvagable materials. The records indicate that after he purchased the materials, he, in turn, sold the cannons to Mr. Isadore Gordon of Rockland, Maine.

When the State of Maine purchased the Fort Knox property in 1923, they learned what had become of the cannons and other equipment. They contacted Mr. Gordon and opened negotiations with him for the sale of the guns and carriages. Finally, an agreement was reached whereby the State of Maine paid two thousand dollars for the equipment he had remaining on his lot.

Thus, the many guns of Fort Knox are to be found in the surrounding towns. Only a few remain at the fort for the thousands of visitors to see and appreciate.

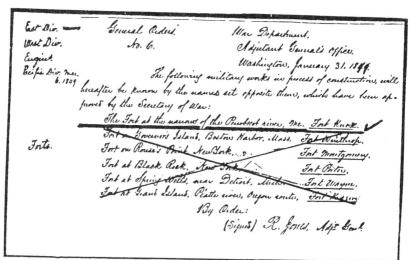

General Order #6, War Department, Washington, D.C., dated January 31, 1849, which gave the official name of FORT KNOX to the Narrows Installation.

TROOPS IN STATION

Civil War

The Civil War touched the State of Maine in four instances, aside from the fine men and distinguished fighting regiments it supplied to General Grant's Union Army.

First was the **_Underground Railroad._** This was the system of people and homes whose assistance to escaping blacks promised them freedom and a new life -- out of slavery. The records do not show very much activity for the operations of the **Underground Railroad** in the State of Maine. Whereas opinions were greatly divided on the subject of slavery in the northern most state in the Union, those who participated in the system did not speak of it nor were many records kept. It was only after years of silence and when the original Underground Railroad operators were dead did information about the system and the buildings involved became known. One fine example of the Underground Railroad is a home located on the banks of the Penobscot River at Brewer, Maine. The Holyoke House at the corner of State Street and North Main Street has a tunnel dug from the house to the river bank. Today, a plaque placed by the Brewer Bi-Centennial Commission commemorates this house and its former activities.

The second incident is directly connected to the first, and this marred the Underground Railroad's long history of success. ***The Parkman Massacre*** was a dark day in the history of the State of Maine during the Civil War. From the scant data than can be put together from limited sources, it seems that a small detatchment of Southern cavalary was spotted in Vermont and making its way to the State of Maine. As the story was told and retold, the Southern unit became larger and larger — until it appeared to be all of General Lee's entire army. Inasmuch as Parkman, Maine was one of the stops on the Underground Railroad system, the citizens thought that the Southern troops were coming for them and that they would all be killed for helping the runaway slaves. According to the story, there were approximately eighteen to two dozen blacks waiting for transportation to be carried to the Canadian border. The local inhabitants felt that if the Southern "army" arrived and found the blacks in their vicinity, it would spell their doom. Rather than risk their own lives, some of the townsmen took it upon themselves to murder the blacks. It seems this was done in a patch of woods outside of town and in their haste, the bodies were not buried. Several days later when the "great Southern army" had not made an appearance, the local clergyman wanted local volunteers to bury the dead. When everyone shrugged their shoulders and refused, he put out a call to fellow clergymen to assist in the burial detail. Ministers from as far away as Bucksport went to Parkman to assist with the burial ceremonies. It was from the records of the Bucksport minister that any details of the **Parkman Massacre** have come to light.

The third incident of the Civil War actually touching the soil of the State of Maine and its citizens was when a Southern officer who was living in Canada's New Brunswick Province planned to rob the bank in Calais, Maine. Fortunately, his clergyman brother, who held a post in the State of Maine, discovered the plan and alerted the military and local authorities. The Southern lieutenant and his accomplices were captured and jailed.

Finally, a Confederate raider sailed into Portland Harbor on June 29, 1863, taking the U. S. Revenue Cutter *Caleb Cushing* to replace their damaged ship. Chase was given and the hijackers were overtaken by two Yankee steamers loaded with armed men. So, the rebel crew sunk the vessel and took to their lifeboats. They were picked up shortly thereafter and made prisoners of war until the conflict ended.

Although Fort Knox was still under construction, the Civil War made it necessary to use the facility as a reserve station and for training purposes.

The first troops arrived at Fort Knox in July, 1863, under the command of Lt. Thomas H. Palmer. The men were elements of the *1st. Maine Heavy Artillery Regiment; 1st. Maine Infantry Volunteers, and the 7th. Maine Infantry Volunteers.* There were a total of twenty-five enlisted men reporting for duty on the first monthly troop return list.

Reinforcements arrived in September, bringing the total compliment of men to fifty-three troopers and one officer.

During the following month, 2nd Lt. James Godfrey was assigned to the fort, and the troop returns listed three deserters. One man was reassigned after completion of his training.

Lt. Palmer took sick during the month of November, although he remained in command. Lt. Godfrey was responsible for keeping the daily operations and drills in the fort functioning smoothly. The monthly report shows Lt. Palmer was still listed on the sick roster throughout December, and another man had deserted.

Lt. James Godfrey was reassigned in February, 1864. During that month, three sergeants were discharged and two more men deserted the post. The report also shows that Doctor A. F. Page, a civilian from Bucksport, was employed by the government as the post physician.

The troop returns for March, 1864, showed that members of the 1st. Maine Heavy Artillery; 1st. Maine Infantry Volunteers; 7th. Maine Infantry Volunteers, and the 21st. Maine Infantry Volunteers were undergoing training and manning Fort Knox. There were a total of twenty-seven enlisted men and one officer. Lt. Palmer was still in command. For the

Hot Shot Furnace. These structures were located near the shore batteries and were used to heat the cannon balls to a white hot color before they were fired at enemy ships.

Captain Daniel Chaplin of the 1st. Maine Heavy Artillery,
one of the units which trained at Fort Knox prior to being
sent forward to the battlefield.

General Joshua L. Chamberlain of Brewer, Maine, was the
Commander of the famed 20th Maine Regiment, whose valor
and courage won the Congressional Medal of Honor, thh
country's highest military award, for the general.

Torpedo Storage Shed. The last structure built at Fort Knox for storing the buoyant floating mines.

remainder of the year, no changes of any significance appeared in the monthly troop reports.

January, 1865, saw only two units quartered at the fort — *1st. Maine Heavy Artillery, and the 7th. Maine Infantry Volunteers* — the other men, having completed their training, were reassigned to active units in the field.

Lt. Thomas Palmer was relieved as the post commander on March 15, 1865. He was assigned to the Maine Coast Defenses Command in Portland.

Lt. George S. Smiley of the Maine Coast Guard (not the same unit as the seagoing organization of today) assumed command of the garrison the same day. The troop returns showed a total of thirty-five men at the post.

Nine more men arrived in April, and with them, a new commanding officer, Lt. George H. Boardman. Lt. Smiley returned to his former post at Portland Harbor.

Lt. Boardman served as the garrison C.O. for less than two months as Captain Charles F. King and Company D of the Maine Coast Guard came to the fort. Captain King was the new commanding officer and the troop returns listed one hundred and sixteen men on duty at Fort Knox.

Members of the *1st. Maine Heavy Artillery; 1st.*

Maine Infantry Volunteers, and the Maine Coast Guard Defense, a total compliment of one hundred and seventeen men garrisoned the post during July and August, 1865.

The following month, Captain John A. McDonnell became the new post commander, and the troop returns listed only seventy-three men in station. Whereas the other troopers had completed their training, they were sent in small detachments to garrison outlying defensive positions located in Belfast, Camden, Sullivan, Castine, and Rockland.

By November, 1865, the fort had only five men listed as on duty in the monthly troop returns.

1st. Lt. Guy Henry of the *1st. United States Army Unit* took command of the installation in January, 1866. Only the members of the Corps of Engineers remained at the fort to complete the construction already in progress.

Bakery with dutch oven.

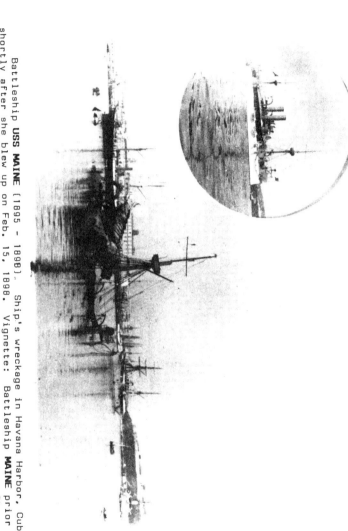

Battleship **USS MAINE** (1895 - 1898). Ship's wreckage in Havana Harbor, Cuba, shortly after she blew up on Feb. 15, 1898. Vignette: Battleship **MAINE** prior to her loss in upper left corner.
Credit: U.S. Navy Photo

Spainish–American War

This was America's shortest war in terms of actual conflict. The general purpose of waging war against Spain was the liberation of Cuba from Spanish rule. Reforms had been promised the Cuban people twenty years earlier. However, the brutal treatment of the Cubans by Spanish military forces and the extensive property damage to U. S. investments aroused the American people in 1895. Both President Grover Cleveland and President William McKinley opposed any U. S. action even though Cuban independence had gained great support in the United States Congress.

An attempt was made in 1897 to settle the conflict, but the Spanish concessions were few and the insurgents wanted complete independence. In December, 1897, the two year old battleship **U.S.S. MAINE** was sent to the port of Havana to protect U.S. citizens and property. The ship was sunk on the night of February 15, 1898, by a tremendous explosion. Two hundred and sixty-six American lives were lost. United States sentiments favored war when news reports stated that the **Battleship MAINE** had been sabotaged.

President McKinley approved a Congressional resolution on April 20th calling for the immediate withdrawal of all Spanish troops from Cuba. Four days later, Spain declared war on the United States. The U. S. Congress declared that hostilities had existed between the United States of America and the Government of Spain the day after President McKinley informed the Spanish to leave Cuba. This official word was issued from the White House on April 25, 1989.

The major portion of the Spanish fleet was anchored at Manila Bay in the Philippines. Commodore George Dewey, commander of the United States Navy's Pacific Squadron, sailed into Manila Harbor on May 1st, attacking and destroying the Spanish fleet. Not one Spanish vessel succeeded in leaving its anchorage.

Two months later to the day, United States troops had surrounded the city of Santiago de Cuba. On July 3rd, Admiral Pascual Topete and his Spanish fleet tried to break out of the U. S. blockade of Santiago Harbor. The Spanish naval squadron was destroyed. The city of Santiago surrendered to United States forces under the command of General William R. Shafter. The Spanish government requested a cease fire and a peace settlement on July 18, 1898.

The peace treaty was signed in Paris, France, on December 10, 1898. Spain relinquished Cuba and ceded to the United States, the Philippine Islands, Guam, and the Mariana Islands — all in the Pacific Ocean — and Puerto Rico in the Carribean.

After Admiral Dewey's great victory in crushing Spain's Pacific naval squadron, people up and down the Atlantic Coast were seeing a Spanish *ghost* fleet, or a Spanish battleship with all guns blazing entering their harbor. The good people of Boston had been sending their valuables and securities to Worcester and to Springfield until the safe deposit vaults in those places were taxed to their utmost. The bankers in those cities placed an ad in the Boston newspapers stating that they had no more available space in their banks for any goods whatsoever.

The people of Bangor, Maine, had petitioned the U.S. Congress for protection, and the War Department was, by the middle of May, almost filled with petitions and requests of like import. The government felt that our Atlantic Coast should be protected as Spain had a powerful Atlantic naval fleet. National Guard units from all states were ordered by a Presidential Proclamation to report for national service.

The Connecticut National Guard was one of the few whose citizen soldiers were at the ready when the Governor of Connecticut asked that they report to Camp Haven, Niantic, Connecticut.

Colonel Charles L. Burdett, commander of the *First Regiment, Connecticut Volunteer Infantry,* had his command on station by May 4th. The *First Regiment* consisted of ten companies with a maximum strength of eighty-four men per company. Six companies were ordered dispatched to garrison an unmanned fortification known as Fort Knox, Maine. The remaining companies would be shipped to other important stations in the State of Maine and in New York.

Members of the 1st. Infantry Regiment, Connecticut Volunteers, Company L of Meriden, Connecticut, who were stationed at Fort Knox.

Credit: Meriden Historical Society.

Special Order No. 122 from Headquarters, Department of the East, dated 6, June, 1898, was received at Camp Haven.

1. The following changes of and assignments to station are ordered: --- The Colonel, Headquarters, unassigned field officers and six companies of the First Regiment, Connecticut Volunteer Infantry, now at Niantic, Connecticut, will proceed to and take station at Fort Knox, near Bucksport, Maine.

The order arrived at Camp Haven the following day, however no one knew where Bucksport, Maine was located. Finally, someone in New London reported that Fort Knox was down the river from Bucksport and could only be reached by about a half day's transportation on barges or river steamers. On June 9th, all transportation arrangements were completed by the Quartermaster's Department for the headquarters staff and four companies of the regiment to proceed to Fort Knox, Maine.

The first section of the train arrived at Bucksport at an early hour on the morning on June 10th, carrying the headquarters staff. A second train arrived shortly after with the troops which were quickly disembarked. By this time, the exact location of Fort Knox had been learned. Company H was soon marched onboard the steam ferry boat *H. G. Totten* and crossed the river to Prospect, Maine, where the command was landed. Companies A, D, and G soon followed.

The Colonel decided not to quarter the troops in the old fort, although there was ample room, but selected a spot on the south and west of the fort, just below an old railroad embankment and on a small clearing in the birch woods. The grass was quickly mowed, the camp laid out, and by noon, the company kitchens were located and the cooks were busy preparing dinner. No attempt was made at any tactical layout of the camp, but places were chosen for the headquarters and staff tents and for the officers' street. The tents of the troops were placed where there would be the best chance to preserve the health of the men.

A pioneer company of thirty-two men was organized as a construction unit to build drainage systems, corduroy roads, and flooring for tents. A signal corps was organized and, in a short time, became extremely proficient. The hospital was established in the fort and samples of the well water were taken for immediate analysis. The Quartermaster, Commissary, and other departments found storage for all their supplies in the fort.

Recruits left Hartford, Connecticut, on June 18, 24, and 28, to join the regiment, bringing them up to the strength ordered by the federal government. Company A had one hundred and one men; Company D had one hundred men; Company G had one hundred men, and Company H had ninety-nine men. There were nine officers on the regimental staff. This brought the total compliment to four hundred and nine personnel as reported by the Regimental Adjutant, Captain Jonathan M. Wainwright, forebearer of famed World War II General Jonathan M. Wainwright of the China-Burma-India Campaign.

Lumber was obtained, good storehouses built and tents were floored. The ground all about the camp for a distance of sixty feet was cleared of all trees and undergrowth, and a perfect system of sanitation was adopted and enforced.

Bakers were detailed from the command. They baked some four hundred loaves of bread a day to supply the troops. A detail of three carpenters was made and they remodeled one of the old rooms at the fort with writing desks and library stacks. It also served as a reading room for the men. Wood was cut and fires built in the large open fireplaces, providing a pleasant resort in stormy weather and in the evenings for those men who were off duty.

Orders were issued from the War Department in Washington, D.C., that all troops stationed at forts and fortified places should be instructed in heavy artillery practice. This task was begun at Fort Knox and details from each company were drilled daily on the heavy guns.

On June 29th, a letter arrived from Washington, D.C., ordering the command at Fort Knox to parade in Bangor, Maine on Independence Day — if the trip did not incur any expense to the federal government.

COLONEL CHARLES L. BURDETT
Commanding 1st Regiment, Conn. Vol. Infantry

Col. Charles Burdett, C.O.
1st. Connecticut Infantry
Volunteers, was the ranking
officer of the Connecticut
troops. He served with
distinction and accompanied
his men to Camp Alger where
many of them died from fever.

Captain Bowen was the last
company commander to bring
his command to Fort Knox.
His troops spent the shortest time at the Fort.

Capt. Charles Bowen of Lewiston, Maine,
CO of Company L, Conn. 1st Regiment.

A stand of colors for the regiment was to be presented by the citizens of Hartford, Connecticut, on the Fourth of July at Fort Knox. However, due to the federal orders, Companies A, D, G, and H, together will all officers, except those detailed for special duty, embarked on a steamer for Bangor, arriving in good time to take part in the annual parade. The command was given a hearty reception by the citizens of Bangor. Early in the afternoon, they returned to Bucksport, where a parade was held. Alderman Hansling and Councilman Countryman of the Hartford City Council presented the handsome silk flags to the regiment.

After an extended reconnaissance of the surrounding countryside, a place was found where a two hundred yard rifle range could be established through the woods, after some heavy timber cutting. The pioneer company handled this task, and by early July, the ground was cleared and ready for the construction of butts and targets.

At the same time, notice was received that newly recruited Company L was ordered to report to Fort Knox without arms, uniforms, equipment, and camp equipage. Prompt steps were taken to fix up the two rooms at the fort which had been used as a library and a workshop into barracks. Lumber was obtained and a framework erected so that when the men arrived, they would be comfortable inside. This protection was needed as the nights were considered chilly.

Company L from Meriden, Connecticut, under the command of Captain Charles B. Bower, a native of Lewiston, Maine, reported for duty at Fort Knox on Sunday, July 10th. The company was at full wartime strength with one hundred and seven men.

Officers and men were kept extremely busy during the whole time they were at Fort Knox, learning their many duties as soldiers and anxiously awaiting the time when they might receive orders to be shipped to the battle area in Cuba. A limited number of passes were issued each day, allowing the men to go to Bucksport, and the privilege was not abused. The Connecticut men gained an excellent record for good conduct and were frequently commended by the town officials.

Colonel Burdett obtained a leave of absence for the purpose of traveling to Washington, D.C., to try to get orders which would send the regiment to the fighting front. He felt that his command had been fully trained and was ready to take their places along side their fellows who were already in the battle area. After numerous telegrams to and from Headquarters, Department of the East, Governor's Island, New York, Special Order No. 152, dated 11, July, 1898, was received at Fort Knox.

Pursuant to telegraphic orders from the War Department of the 9th instant, the companies of the First Connecticut, U. S. Volunteer Infantry, will proceed from their present stations in this department, to Camp Haven, Niantic, Connecticut, reporting upon arrival to the regimental commander.

When the regiment shall be asembled at Camp Haven, it will proceed to Camp Russell A. Alger, Virginia, and report to the Commanding General, Second Army Corps, for duty.

The troops will take their entire equipments and be provided with not less than five day's rations on leaving their present stations. Property pertaining to the posts of Fort Knox, Maine, and Great Gull and Plum Island, New York, from which the entire garrisons are to be withdrawn, will be disposed of under the direction of the Chief Quartermaster and Chief Commissary of Subsistence of the department, previous to the departure of the responsible officers.

The Quartermaster's Department will furnish the transportation; the Subsistence Department will arrange for the necessary subsistence.

The travel enjoined is necessary for the public service.

By command of Brigadier-General Gillespie:
GEORGE ANDERWS,
Assistant Adjutant-General.

Official: HERMAN C. SCHUMM,
1st. Lieutenant, 2nd Artillery
Aide-de-Camp.

Five minutes after the delivery of this message,

65

the men broke out with loud cheering, yells, routed out the band and paraded enmasse about the camp. The temporary buildings of brush and saplings that had been built were set on fire, and water had to be thrown on the tents about the edge of the camp to keep them from catching fire. For a short time, pandemonium reigned, with, however, no breach of discipline. The news was received throughout the regiment' with the same satisfaction, and Special Order No. 152 was complied with promptly.

Preparations were made to clear the post and at 4:50 AM, Saturday, 14, July, 1898, those companies of the *First Regiment, Connecticut Volunteer Infantry* stationed at Fort Knox, Maine, were onboard the train heading for their home base. They arrived at Niantic at 9:00 PM that evening.

A lone soldier, Fort Keeper Leopold Hegyi, Ordnance Sergeant, United States Army, lowered the colors at sunset on July 14th. He assumed command of Fort Knox once again. Sergeant Hegyi had been at Fort Knox since 1887. He was now serving in his thirty-first year of military service, eleven years of which had been spent at Fort Knox.

MINING THE NARROWS

The Narrows of the Penobscot River begins below Fort Knox on the westerly side of Orphan Island (now called Verona Island) and ends twenty miles up the river at the Ports of Bangor and Brewer. The channel was deep enough to support the largest vessels of the Spanish Atlantic Squadron in and around the Fort Knox area. The river was very narrow between the mainland and Orphan Island, but widened to make the Port of Bucksport at the northern tip of the island. It narrowed up beyond the Town of Bucksport to a body of water between seven hundred and fifty to over a thousand feet wide in places all the way to the twin cities of Bangor and Brewer. The most vital area was the distance from the northerly tip of Orphan Island to the mouth of Penobscot Bay. Although the water midstream was exceeding deep — able to accommodate the largest vessels afloat in the 1980s — Fort Knox was the only defensive measure against a foreign fleet entering Penobscot Bay and going up the river to capture the commercial cities of Bangor and Brewer.

Whereas hundreds of reports were received by the War Department in Washington about Spanish warships being spotted at various points off the Atlantic Coast, orders were dispatched from Headquarters, Office of the Corps of Engineers, Washington, D.C., to the Commanding Officer, Corps of Engineers,

Scale ¼

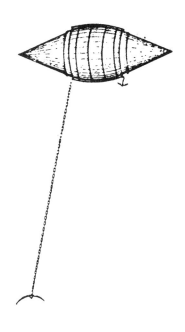

Drawing of the Buoyant Torpedo as
found in government files in 1882.

Buoyant Torpedo. (Floating
Mine). The type used to
mine the Penobscot River
during the Spanish-American

War.   Credit: US Navy.

This was one type of Buoyant
torpedo used in mining the
Penobscot River at Fort Knox.
          Credit: U.S.Army

Submarine Mine Storage Depot, Willet's Point, New York, to ship Buoyant Torpedoes, Types 43 and 32 to Fort Knox, Maine.

A determination was made by the federal government that the old casemated forts would not be able to defend themselves against the armament of the modern naval vessel. The new ten and twelve inch rifled, breech-loading cannon, which were a part of a ship's armament, could fire faster and more accurately than the muzzle-loaded, smoothbore cannons found in all sea coast fortifications. The development of buoyant torpedoes (submarine floating mines) gave an advantage to the old forts and offered open harbors a measure of protection.

The advent of electricity brought forth many developments in the field of explosives. The buoyant torpedo, or submarine floating mine, could be exploded by an electrically discharged fuse placed in the floating head. The unit was usually exploded from a shore installation where the wires from each mine were located. A battery or series of storage batteries were kept fully charged, and as a vessel passed over the submerged explosive, the ordnance sergeant would throw the appropriate switch igniting the charge.

Buoyant torpedo No. 32 was one of the types used at Fort Knox during the Spanish-American War. This submarine mine was constructed from quarter inch thick steel in a spherical shape. It was thirty-two inches in diameter and contained one hundred pounds of dynamite. This mine was designed to be submerged in depths of over forty feet of water. It was held in position by an anchor which was a five hundred pound, 26 inch diameter weight. The submarine floating mine (or buoyant torpedo) was held by a wire mooring rope or cable of a predetermined length. The mooring cables were made up in advance and their length depended upon the depth of water in which the mines were being placed.

There were three types of firing devices used to arm the explosive charge. These detonating fuse boxes were classified as skirmish, judgement, and main line.

The buoyant torpedo loaded with a skirmish detonator was employed for automatic firing only. The charge could be fired by contact with an outside source — such as a ship's hull.

The judgement detonator could only be fired from an above water position.

There were disadvantages to the skirmish and judgement detonating methods. The skirmish loaded buoyant torpedo could allow an enemy to sail an old vessel over a mined area thereby clearing a passage through the mine field. The skirmish unit was also dangerous to friendly shipping.

The judgement detonator was almost useless in foggy weather, and on black, starless nights when vessels could not be seen or identified as friend or foe. It would be very embarrassing if the vessel recently blown up on a foggy night proved to be a friendly.

The main line firing system was preferable, as it was a combination of both contact and surface detonation. With three wires leading from the main line fuse box, the ordnance sergeant controlling the detonation of the mines could select if he wanted the mine to explode on contact or by his own hand.

The ground torpedo was a smaller version of the buoyant torpedo, being twenty-eight inches in diameter and packed with two hundred pounds of explosives. This submarine mine was planted in less than forty feet of water and had an extremely powerful underwater explosion. The large dynamite charge sent off shattering shock waves which could wrack a ship's hull causing the riveted plates to buckle or a wooden ship's planking to spring leaks.

Major Richard L. Hoxie, Corps of Engineers, was the officer-in-charge of the coast defenses for the State of Maine and New Hampshire. The project for the torpedo defense for the State of Maine included the mining of the Penobscot and Kennebec Rivers and Portland Harbor.

During April, 1898, mines were placed in the three channels leading into Portland Harbor. Early in May, the mouth of the Kennebec and the Narrows of the Penobscot River was mined with buoyant explosives. The submarine mines had been placed in position as part of the defense of the Penobscot River at and above Fort Knox, and the troops stationed at the fort were there for the purpose of guarding these mines as well as manning the garrison.

The wires connected to the mines were led into a casemate in the lower part of the fort where electric batteries were established by means of which the mines could be exploded. There were strict regulations regarding the use of the channel where the mines were placed and patrol boats were stationed both above and below the defense. These patrol boats guided the coastal schooners and fishermen through the mine field and kept other boats, that did not know the Narrows were mined, from being accidently blown up and sunk.

The officer commanding Fort Knox had supervision over the entire operation including the mine field even though it was under the direct supervision of the United States Engineer Corps. The Mine Engineering Officer gave instructions to the commanding officer of Fort Knox about the handling of the mines.

The Ordnance Sergeant at Fort Knox is in charge of the mining casemate and is instructed in respect to turning on the batteries when the mines are to be made ready for the approach of an enemy. He is instructed to report to you for orders in such

72

emergency and to permit no one except yourself
to have access to the mining casemates.

R. HOXIE,
Chief of Mining Engineers.

Fortunately, the war with Spain ended without the men at Fort Knox having to fire upon an enemy. The navy minesweepers steamed up the Penobscot River during August, 1898, and removed all the mines. The materials were cleaned and stored, the explosives being removed from the mines and afterwards utilized in connection with rock excavation for fortifications being constructed in the district.

More than a year later, Major S. W. Roessler, the engineering officer at Fort Knox, submitted a plan for the construction of a permanent torpedo storehouse to be built near the shore. A three thousand dollar appropriation was requested for the construction of the storehouse on December 8, 1899. Five days later, General John M. Wilson, Chief of Engineers, U.S. Army, Washington, D.C., replied personally to Major Roessler's request, informing him that the appropriations for *Torpedoes for Harbor Defense* were exhausted and that the question of construction would be deferred until a new appropriation became available.

Major Roessler received a welcomed letter within days after the end of the govenment's fiscal year. On July 13, 1900, the major was informed that his request for funds to build a torpedo storehouse had been approved and that construction could begin. The storehouse was completed the following year and has remained intact for more than eight-nine years.

THE LONE GUARDIAN

Ordnance Sergeant Leopold Hegyi
United States Army

FORT KNOX — the military garrison at the Narrows of the Penobscot River in the town of Prospect, Maine, — was the place called home for thirteen long and lonely years to Ordnance Sergeant Leopold Hegyi, (pronounced Heg-eye), a thirty-three year veteran of the United States Army. Fort Knox had been Sergeant Hegyi's permanent residence since 1887. He was the Fort Keeper — the non-commissioned officer responsible for maintaining and guarding the government's property. This trusted position could only be filled by a special human being, and Leopold Hegyi was just such a man.

Can you imagine what life on a 125-acre deserted military installation was like before the turn of the century? The reservation stretched from the peak of the summit, located to the rear of the fort, down to the river's edge. The fort itself had not undergone any major repairs since 1869.

You woke at day break, washed, dressed, cooked breakfast, walked down to the fort and raised the flag, started a new daily report, then made a tour of inspection. There was not a single human voice to greet you while making your daily rounds. A few

birds took flight from their nests when they heard your footsteps echo loudly on the great granite floor. Small animals and rodents scurried at your approach. Your lantern cast weird shadows on the walls. There was no canteen available so you could drop in for a hot cup of coffee, a doughnut, or tobacco for your pipe. There was no P.X. (Post Exchange) enabling you to purchase writing paper, personal items, or a glass of beer. You entered your inspection tour in the daily report, noted any changes in anything that might appear to be different from the pervious day, then returned to your little house and prepared an early lunch.

You walked down to the Ferry Store at noon, waiting for the boat to carry you across the river to Bucksport. At last you heard another human voice and was able to talk with other people.

You proceeded directly to the post office upon arriving in Bucksport to pick up any dispatches which may have been sent from Heaquarters, Fort Preble, Portland, or maybe one directly from Headquarters, Department of the East, Washington, D.C., notifying the Fort Keeper of a pending inspection. There may even have been a letter from your wife back in Brooklyn, New York, informing you as to when she would be making her semi-annual visit.

You would make another tour of inspection before sunset, hearing the same animal noises, walking in the same footsteps as on the previous day — doing exactly the same thing over and over and over. You saluted the flag, lowered it, folded it neatly, then walked across the rampart to your quarters.

Leopold Hegyi was born in Pesth, (now Budapest), Hungary on February 29, 1832 — a Leap Year.

NOTE: There is now some question as to whether Sgt, Hegyi was born in 1832 or 1829. None of his available military records lists an actual year of birth, only a month and day. The 1832 date was derived at by the age given by Sgt. Hegyi on a military document. Subtracting this given age from the date appearing on the document was how the 1832 birth date was affixed. Suffice it to say that he was born between 1829 and 1832.

Little is known of his formative years when he grew up in the twin cities of Buda and Pest before they became united. It is suspected that Leopold had a general, but good, education, and that he emigrated to the United States sometime after the anti-Harpsburg Revolution (1848 - 1850). Like most other Hungarians who came to America following the revolution, Hegyi landed in New York. Leopold was probably between 18 and 21 years of age when he arrived. From the best information that is available, he settled with the Hungarian community in Brooklyn.

It can only be assumed that Hegyi was employed in a livery stable or had worked with horses in Hungary, as he was very knowledgable about the animals. When he joined the United States Army on October 4, 1867, his first assignment was to the General Mounted Service at the St. Louis Depot, St. Louis, Missouri.

Leopold Hegyi accomplished a feat during his first five year enlistment which few enlisted men have achieved. He was promoted to the non-commissioned rank of First Sergeant — one of the highest non-commissioned ranks in the U.S. Army. Throughout his long military career, Sergeant Leopold Hegyi was given an excellent rating; he was a professional soldier and an excellent soldier.

Sgt. Hegyi spent the next twenty years' of his life in St. Louis training young soldiers for the United States Cavalry.

After his initial hitch at the St. Louis Depot, he was transferred to **Jefferson Barracks,** also located in Missouri. During the next fifteen years (or three army hitches), Hegyi instructed men who would serve with General George Armstrong Custer's famed 7th. Cavalry. When he reenlisted on October 4, 1887, his job of teaching the basics of horsemanship to the youthful recruits, who would be fighting the **Plains Indian Wars** at numerous far-flung western outposts, was over. He would be traveling back to the East Coast to be reassigned and stationed at Fort Knox, Maine.

Apparently, having accumulated leave time, Leopold stopped in New York to visit friends. He

The **Totten Ferry**, the craft used at Bucksport, Maine to transport men and equipment across the Penobscot River to the Prospect Ferry Store, near the fort.

Prospect Ferry Store where Sergeant Hegyi visited each day for one beer and pleasant conversation.

either met his future wife Louise at this time, or a marriage was arranged for him — as was the old world custom. Little information could be found about Mrs. Louise Hegyi or about when the couple were married. However, when the sergeant took up his new duty post at Fort Knox, Maine, it is known that his wife did not accompany him to his new duty station in the State of Maine.

It must have been somewhat disappointing to 1st. Sergeant Leopold Hegyi when he looked over the deserted garrison for the first time. It was in a state of disrepair —— windows were broken out —— roofs leaking —— rooms piled high with debris. He walked across the parade grounds looking at the massive granite structure. This impressed him greatly; he often remarked about the fine quality workmanship. It was like the very best work done in Europe.

He toted his luggage up the spiral stariway, which would become so familiar to him during the next thirteen years. He walked over the rampart, going to his quarters on the far side of the compound. There stood the small, wood-framed house, which would be Leopold Hegyi's home for the next long and lonely thirteen years.

When his daily military duties at the fort had been completed, Sgt. Hegyi would walk down the steep embankment to the river —— the site of the Prospect Ferry Store. He was a daily visitor. Here, at last, he had the opportunity to hear another human voice, and to be able to talk with other people. Everyone was his friend. They admired the tall, stately, uniformed sergeant with his wide-brimmed cavalry hat and shiny black boots.

Leopold's bluish-grey eyes were always alert and sparkling; his iron-grey hair and white beard were always well trimmed; his uniform was clean and impeccable, and those tall, black, cavalry boots glistened as they were polished nightly. His conversation was light, but interesting, as Leopold was a well read man. His personal library in his quarters contained over 190 volumes. Combine all this with study and the fact he had been born in Hungary, traveled across Europe to come to America, had lived in New York and served 20 years in St. Louis — the gateway to the Wild West — his experiences alone were marvels and wonders to the locals whose lives were spent in and around Penobscot Bay for the most part.

Sgt. Hegyi allowed himself one glass of beer per day. He would sip his beer, talk with his friends, and when he was ready to go back to the fort, he would say, *"Now, I've got to go the hill up."*

Mrs. Louise Hegyi would make the long train journey from New York City to visit her husband at Fort Knox twice a year. Whereas both were advanced in years, and Mrs. Hegyi over the child-bearing stage, she traveled with her two small dogs. Her usual visit was for two weeks, and she boarded at the home of Edwin W. Grindle rather than stay in the sergeant's quarters at the fort. The Grindle girls, Mildred and Lucy, entertained the dogs until one of them snapped at Lucy causing some fear. She would not have anything to do with them after that.

Mildred's recollections of Sgt. Hegyi were how nice a man he was and of how he visited the family home. It seemed that Mrs. Hegyi was pleasant, but somewhat distant. She described Mrs. Hegyi as having sharp features with a hawk-like nose. Her eyes were dark and small. Her manner was strange and quiet and Mildred could not remember Mrs. Hegyi smiling too often. Perhaps it was the European nature.

As further proof of his genuine love for horses, the old sarge kept one in the stable at Bucksport. During the winter months he exercised the horse on the ice when the river was frozen. Whereas he did not own a sleigh or sled, he took an ordinary wooden sawhorse and attached skis to the legs. He would straddle the sawhorse and ride this unique conveyance over the ice.

Leopold Hegyi was promoted to the rank of Ordnance Sergeant, United States Army, on November 22, 1888. It was the second highest non-commissioned officers rank in the U.S. Army. Only a Sergeant-Major outranked him.

Sgt. Hegyi received a dispatch from Headquarters, Fort Preble, Portland, informing him that Colonel Hughes of the Inspector General's Office in Washington,

D.C., would arrive in August to inspect the garrison. The Colonel's report about Sergeant Hegyi is presented in full.

Bucksport, Maine, August 30, 1897
The Inspector General, U.S. Army
Through Hdqrs. Depart. of the East
Washington, D.C.

Sir:

I respectfully submit the following report of the biennial inspection of Fort Knox, Maine. Ordnance Sergeant Leopold Hegyi is still in charge. He is looking quite feeble and informs me that he is sixty-eight years of age. I understand from him that in the month of October next, he will have served thirty years. It is my conviction that, when the time has arrived when the law will permit this old soldier to lay down his responsibilities by being transferred to the retired list, he should be so transferred. I think the interest of the service will not suffer by so doing, and I also think that it would be better for the sergeant if he were relieved from duty here and would go and spend the remainder of his days with his family in Brooklyn ----------.

Respectfully submitted,

R. P. Hughes,
Colonel, Inspector General

The Inspector General made his observations and feelings quite clear. Sergeant Leopold Hegyi was getting old and the loneliness of his duty station was taking its toll on the human body and mind. However, it is apparent that Headquarters did not act upon Colonel Hughes' recommendations as Hegyi was reenlisted for a period of three years at Fort Preble, Portland, on October 4, 1897 — a hitch he would not complete.

Captain Thomas Ward of the Inspector General's Office made an earlier inspection of the ungarrisoned post of Fort Knox, Maine. In part, his report reads:

---- *The storm doors and windows on the north side of the house occupied by the Ordnance Sergt. are necessary ---- that the roof on the south side needs reshingling; new floors and general repairs are needed at a probable cost not to exceed two hundred dollars.*

---- *further stated that the roof inside the fort used as Ordnance Storeroom leaks and requires attention.*

The United States found itself at war with Spain. Ordnance Sergeant Leopold Hegyi received a communique from Headquarters, Department of the East, Washington, D.C., stating that Fort Knox would be garrisoned by elements of the *First Regiment of Infantry, Connecticut Volunteers, Colonel Burdett commanding.* At long last, the fort would be manned. Not only did the Connecticut Infantry come to Fort Knox, but U.S. Naval Forces were also present. Mine laying vessels and navy patrol craft placed buoyant torpedoes (submarine mines) above and below Fort Knox in the Penobscot River. Fortunately, the war with Spain was the shortest conflict ever fought by this Nation.

By the end of fall, all the troops had departed; the mines had been removed, deactivated, and stored at the fort, and the Navy sailed away. Fort Knox was quiet again.

1900

A New Year and a New Century

Nothing much had changed at Fort Knox, especially in the life of Fort Keeper Leopold Hegyi.

The Corps of Engineers submitted plans for the construction of a Torpedo Storehouse down near the shore, but the plans had not been approved. The Army said they did not have any money. Nevertheless, Leopold Hegyi was not feeling very well. Each day it became more difficult for him to make his daily tour of inspection.

On July 16, when one of the local fishermen noticed that the flag was not flying from the fort, he investigated and found Sergeant Hegyi extremely ill. He sent word to the fort's physician, Doctor W. F. Putnam in Bucksport that Sergeant Hegyi was very ill and requested him to come immediately.

The doctor proceeded to the fort on the next ferry boat only to find the old sarge unconscious.

He sent the following letter to Headquarters, U.S. Corps of Engineers, Portland:

Maj. Roessler

> *U. S. Engineers*
> *Portland, Me.*

Sir:

> *I have to inform you that Serg't Leopold Hegyi of Fort Knox cannot survive but a few hours. He was taken with an attack of apoplexy Sat. A.M., and is now unconcious. I have engaged Mr. Jas. Pierce, a veteran of the Civil War, and Mr. Geo. Bennett, a trusty young man, to take care of him and to look out for gov't property. Both men live in the immediate vicinity and are worthy citizens. I knew of no other course to pursue ------.*

> *Most resp'y*
> *W. F. Putnam, M.D.*
> *Physician & Surgeon*

Bucksport
7/16/00

Mrs. Hegyi was notified of her husband's condition immediately. She left New York and arrived at the fort the following day. Her husband was dead.

Ordnance Sergeant Leopold Hegyi died at 6:35 P.M. on July 17, 1900.

Thomas H. Jackson, 2nd. Lieutenant, U.S. Corps of Engineers, was sent from Fort Preble, Portland, to represent the government. He arrived on July 18th, and being the only officer present and available, he took the inventory of Sergenat Hegyi's personal effects. Whereas Mrs. Hegyi was at the fort, the property was turned over to her. She signed for the sergeant's back pay and his personal belongings, then left for the return trip to New York.

Fort Knox, Maine
July 19, 1900

I have this day received from 2nd Lieut. Thos. H. Jackson, Corps of Engineers, U.S.A., the following articles, being the personal effects of Ordnance Sergeant Leopold Hegyi, deceased on the 17th instant, at Fort Knox, Maine:

Personal Library	*volumes*
Self-Interpreting Bible	*3*
American Encyclopedic Dictionary	*4*
Library of Universal History	*8*
Encyclopedia Britannica	*25*
International Library of Famous Authors	*20*
Great Commanders	*13*

Stoddard's Lectures	10
Webster's Dictionary	1
Century Dictionary	10
History of the World	9
Abbott's Histories	32
Americanized Encyclopedic Britannica	10
America's Wonderland	8
Century Dictionary	1
Photographic Scenes	1
Miscellaneous Works	44

Personal Items

1 Sofa; 1 Music Box; 8 Chairs; 4 Tables; 1 Ice Box; 2 Stands; 2 Setteens; 1 Mirror; 3 Lamps; 1 Clock; 1 Bedroom Set; 6 Cooking Utensils; 20 Dishes; 1 Sabre, and 3 Suits of Clothing.

Money Due Soldier:

17 days pay from June 30 to July 17, 1900
For 30 years continuous service, $7.00 per month
For clothing not drawn in kind, $114.33

s/ Louise Hegyi
_____

Widow of the deceased

The above list is not too great when it covers thirty-three years of a man's life spent in the United States Army.

Ordnance Sergeant Leopold Hegyi, United States Army, Fort Keeper, Fort Knox, Maine, 1832 - 1900, was buried in the **Narrows Cemetery,** Sandy Point, Maine.

His plot was donated by the Bennett Family, who had become friends with Sergeant Hegyi over the years he served at the fort. Sadly it must be noted that a grateful government did not afford a thirty-three year veteran of the military a choice last resting place. The entrance to the Narrows Cemetery is directly off the main road and it falls sharply away down a steep incline toward the river bank. Sergeant Hegyi's grave lies at the very foot of the cemetery over in the right hand corner by a fallen down wire fence. A cluster of cedar trees have grown up, shading the grave, and drawing much moisture to and around it. Behind the fence is much debris from those who use sacred ground as a sporting and drinking spot.

The grave marker has sunken into the ground now (May, 1990) and it is slanting to the rear of the grave. The narrow marker is stained and water-marked. It bears only the following inscription: **ORD. SGT. LEOPOLD HEGYI, USA.** No dates. No nothing.

This is not a very fitting end for a man who gave half of his life to his adopted country in the service of the United States Army.

THE LAST DAYS

Upon the death of Sgt. Leopold Hegyi in 1900, the U. S. Army ordered other ordnance sergeants to be assigned to Fort Knox, guarding and tending to the government's property.

Sgt. John O'Rouke was the first non-commissioned officer to assume command of the fort. He did have some companionship in 1900 and 1901. During the summer months, personnel from the Army Corps of Engineers and civilian workmen were at the fort constructing the torpedo storehouse near the wharf area by the river. When the torpedo shed was completed, he, like Sgt. Hegyi before him, walked the empty galleries and ramparts alone. Occasionally, the old sergeant would have "visitors" during the night.

According to the late Chief Justice Raymond Fellows, in a speech delivered on August 1, 1949, during the Fort Knox Centennial,

"In those days, in order to irritate and annoy the sergeant, the sixteen year old boys of Bucksport often visited the fort after dark and captured it."

Sgt. O'Rouke would raise the flag each morning and take it down each night. He did this day after day without fail. Of course, there was always reams of government forms and paperwork which had to be filled out.

Sgt. Jack Merideth relieved Sgt. O'Rouke. He did not find his duties any more strenuous than those of his predecessors. However, he was able to talk with the many people who drove their carriages or motor cars to see the fort. He could see the people who were traveling to and from Bangor on the old Boston steamships. Life was not that unbearable just prior to and following World War I at the garrison for the Fort Keeper.

Sergeant Edwards arrived at Fort Knox in mid-1923. He, among the ordnance sergeant Fort Keepers, was probably the most fortunate. His tenure of service lasted less than three months. Fort Knox had been declared excess to the government's needs and was to be sold.

Dwight F. Davis, the assistant Secretary of War, notified Governor Percival P. Baxter of Maine that Fort Knox was for sale.

October 12, 1923

My dear Governor: - The Congress of the United States by legislation approved March 4, 1923 (Public No. 501, 67th Congress), has authorized the Secretary of War to dispose of military reservations including

that known as Fort Knox, opposite the town of
Bucksport on the Penobscot River, Maine. The
reservation contains 124.7 acres of land with
improvements thereon consisting of an old brick and
granite fortification and a few buildings.

The Fort Knox reservation has been duly appraised
in accordance with the provisions of the above quoted
legislation, in four parcels, as follows:

Tract No. 1

25 acres of land, more or less	$100.00
Improvements thereon consisting of an	
Old Fort and brick storehouse	1.00

Tract No. 2

5 acres of land, more or less	100.00
Improvements thereon	650.00

Tract No. 3

35 acres of land, more or less	35.00
150 cords of mixed timber thereon	300.00

Tract No. 4

60 acres of land, more or less	60.00
350 cords of mixed timber thereon	876.00

Total	**$2,121.00**

You are hereby notified that the appraisal of the foregoing property, both as a whole and in parcels, with the improvements thereon, have been approved by me on October 2, 1923, in the amount of $2,121.00. While the legislation in question provides that the state or the county or municipality in which the property is located shall be entitled to a period of six months from the date of the approval of said appraisal in which to exercise the option contained in the above Section 3 of the Act of March 4, 1923, I shall deem it a favor to be advised of the decision of the state, county, or municipality in this matter if such can be reached before the expiration of the time provided by law. It is presumed in this connection that if the state does not desire the property you will take the matter up with the county or municipality.

Any information or data which may be of assistance to you in this respect will be gladly furnished upon request.

> Sincerely yours,
> Dwight F. Davis,
> The Assistant Secretary of War.

Governor Baxter contacted the State Treasurer instructing him to forward to the War Department the required sum to purchase Fort Knox for the State of Maine.

A deed was issued on December 4, 1923, to the State of Maine, by John W. Weeks, the Secretary of War. The last paragraph is one of interest in this deed. It reads:

To have and to hold the above described premises unto the party of the second part (the State of Mainé) forever for use for public purposes only. It is expressly understood that upon cessation of such use, the title and the right of possession to the property hereinbefore described shall revert to the United States without notice, demand, or action brought.

Fort Knox can be used for no other purpose than to serve the public.

June 9, 1924

For and in behalf of the State of Maine, I hereby acknowledge to have received from the Commanding Officer, Portland Harbor, Fort Williams, Maine, the following described tract or parcel of land with all improvements thereon, situate in the town of Prospect, County of Knox (formerly Lincoln County), State of Maine, being all of the land known as Fort Knox, conveyed to the United States of America by deed dated the 4th day of December, 1923.

STATE OF MAINE
by/Percival P. Baxter
Governor of Maine.

Thus, after being under the control of the federal government for eighty years, Fort Knox passed into the hands of the people of the State of Maine. However, it was not until 1940 that the fort came

Governor Percival Baxter of Maine did not hesitate to
purchase Fort Knox when the government offered it for sale.

under the jurisdicition of the Maine Parks Commission.

It is interesting to note the description given the fort by Assistant Secretary of War Davis in his letter to Governor Baxter —*an old brick and granite fortification and a few out buildings. Value $1.00.*

Six days prior to Assistant Secretary Davis' description of Fort Knox, Mr. Harry W. Reynolds wrote a picture of his visit to the fort, which appeared in the **Boston Transcript** newspaper on Saturday, October 6, 1923.

There is no limit for appreciation and thrill in walking through the rifle galleries and parade ground and casemates, parapets, moats, and a score of other fascinating features.

Phlegmatic souls who know neither victory or defeat as Teddy (President Theodore Roosevelt) would have it, can gather little from such visits, but those fortunate enough to be possessed of sentiment a-plenty may obtain no end of inspiration and pleasure in browsing about the fort.

That the person who drafted the plans for Fort Knox was assisted by able engineers is evidenced by examination of the masonry. My eyes were indeed opened to a realization of what fine masonry is --- when I saw virtually all the pointing in as perfect condition as the day it was put there over fifty years ago. Great white beautiful slabs of granite placed

edge on edge with the exactest precision and care.
And, the brick work was the same.

The finest pieces of workmanship in the whole
structure are the spiral staircases in which a complete
circular colume is formed by the several treads and
risers, which are of solid pieces of granite. Of the
many guns placed at Knox during the Civil War, only
a few remain; the others have been given as souvenirs
to different parks, armories, and other organizations.

Near both the north and south shore batteries
may still be seen the brick ovens where the forty-two
pound cannon balls were heated. It's very delightful
along the shore where the cedar trees have grown
up and hidden the guns. Nature has a kindly way
of protecting objects when they become embarrassed
by disuse........

There appears to be a great difference of opinion
between the Army's description of Fort Knox and
that of a visitor. Hopefully, visitors to this magnificent
fortification will see it through the same pair of
eyes as Mr. Reynolds did in 1923: — that you can
look at the marvelous granite and masonry work
reflecting back to the time when the builders of Fort
Knox received a dollar a day for labor and up to $3.00
per day for craftsmen such as stonecutters, quarrymen,
and master masons.

When you look at the empty gun positions, think
back to a day in 1865 when this mighty bastion of

defense bristled with two hundred and fifty cannons, and 101 year old William Hutchins was saluted with a thundering salvo as he sailed passed the installation. Hutchins, a resident of the town of Penobscot, was one of the last two survivors of the Revolutionary War. He was taken onboard a United States Revenue Cutter (forerunner of the U. S. Coast Guard) at his home, carried up the Penobscot River passed Fort Knox for a celebration in his honor given by the City of Bangor. Vice President of the United States Hannibal Hamlin was the guest speaker for the day's events. As the Revenue Cutter steamed passed Fort Knox, the old fort's great Rodman guns gave a salute to the old soldier who was standing on the ship's bridge. The resounding roar caused many windows to shatter across the river in Bucksport.

The salute of 1883, during the Bucksport Fourth of July celebration, was the last great salvo fired from the fort's many cannons. Soldiers from Fort Williams, Portland, were transported to Fort Knox to mann and fire the weapons. Again, all windows not open in Bucksport and Verona Island (the new and present name given Orphan Island) were either cracked or broken.

Fort Knox is an emblem of peace. It is and has always been a peaceful fort. But, it is also an emblem of solid preparedness. It looks like protection.

These United States of America must be protected — for not only the lives of our own people, but civilization itself depends upon this Nation's safety.

Fort Knox — a monument to preparedness and to peace.

GLOSSARY

ABRASION: Wearing or rubbing away such as the inner core of a cannon barrel as the projectile is fired through it.

AMMUNITION: The projectile discharged from any firearm or the explosive package used to discharge a projectile.

ARCHES: Curved or bow-like structure spanning an opening such as in a wall of a fort.

ARTILLERY, MOUNTAIN: Cannon light enough to be hauled or packed by animals to extremely high elevations.

BANQUETTE: A platform or bank behind a parapet on which soldiers may stand and fire their weapons.

BARBETTE: An earth platform for cannon.

BARRACKS: A building or group of buildings to house soldiers.

BASTION: A fortified position which is the projecting portion of a rampart.

BATTERY: Specific guns or cannons placed in a group for heavy firepower.

BREVET: A commission advancing an officer

in honorary rank without advances in pay or in command.

CALIBER: The internal diameter of a cannon's or gun's barrel or the weight and diameter of the weapon's projectile.

CANISTER: A metalic cylinder fired from a cannon.

CANISTER SHOT: A projectile that is designed to explode and spray metal fragments over a wide area.

CAPONNIER: A cut out or earth dug away being readied for an emplacement for firearms and/or cannon.

CAPT.: Abbreviation for the military rank of Captain.

CARRIAGE, FRONT PINTLE: A wheeled frame for carrying a heavy cannon with a pin in the rear axel which allowed the unit to pivot from side to side.

CARTRIDGE: Any casing of metal containing a charge of powder for a firearm or the projectile discharged by an explosion.

CARTRIDGE BAG: A cloth or leather container for the metal projectiles to be used in a firearm.

CASEMATE: A bombproof shelter, as in a fortification, for guns and men.

CASTING: That which is formed in a mold.

CLERK: A worker in an office who is charged with the care of records and correspondence.

DEMIBASTION: A half unit or small fortified position built off a rampart.

DITCH: A long, narrow trench or channel dug in the ground surrounding a fortification, sometimes filled with water.

DRAINAGE: A system to draw off water thereby making a land area dry.

EMPLACEMENT: The position assigned to guns or to a battery within a fortification.

ENBARBETTE: A platfort or elevation of earth from which cannons may be fired over a parapet.

FACADES: The front or principal face of a fortification.

FENDERS: A soft material, usually held by a rope and hung over wharves to protect boats from damage while docking or being tied up to a dock.

FIELD GUN: A cannon so mounted as to be freely movable and suitable for use with troops in the battlefield.

FIELD PIECE: Any portable weapon, hand held or horse drawn, used in the combat area.

FLANK: The right or left positions of a fort

or a formation of soldiers.

FORT KEEPER: The soldier, usually a top-grade sergeant, in charge of a vacant fortification.

FUSE: A length of combustible material passing into an explosive charge designed to be lit to ignite the charge. Later, electricity was used to ignite the internal fuses in explosive charges.

GALLERY: A tunnel or underground passage or a long, narrow enclosed area. In a fort, they were rifle galleries.

GARRISON: A place or fortification for troops. The military force stationed in a fort or town.

GLACIS: A slope that runs downward from a fortification.

GUNS, FRONT PINTLE: Cannons mounted on wheeled carriages with the pin in the front axel capable of pivoting to fire over a large area.

GUNPOWDER: An explosive mixture used as a propellant in firearms and cannon.

HEAVY PIECE: Military term used to describe large cannon.

HOT SHOT: Solid cannon balls which have been heated prior to being discharged.

HOT SHOT FURNACE: Brick structure in which cannon balls are heated before firing.

LT. & LIEUT.: Abbreviation for the military ank of lieutenant.

LT.-COL.: Abbreviation for the military rank of lieutenant-colonel.

MAGAZINE: A storage area or building to house arms, ammunitions and explosives.

MAJ.: Abbreviation for the military rank of major.

MASTIC: The resin obtained from a specific evergreen tree used in varnishes.

MINIWORK: A constructed portion of a fortification outside the main fort, such as an outlying gun battery.

MUZZLE: The front end of the barrel of a firearm.

ORDNANCE: Military weapons, cannons or explosives.

OUTWORKS: Any outer defensive position laying beyond the ditch of a fort.

OVERSEER: One who superintends a work project.

PARADE GROUNDS: A ground, area or field where military drills, reviews and maneuvers are held.

PARCHMENT: (military): A special waterproof

paper used to wrap explosive materials.

PENTAGON: Any object which has five sides and five angles, or a five-sided building such as Fort Knox.

PLATFORM: Any floor or flat surface raised above the adjacent level to mount cannon or military hardware.

POKER: A metal rod for stirring a fire.

POSTS: Buildings, grounds, or a place occupied by a detachment of military personnel.

POSTERN: A small back gate or door in a fortification.

PROJECTILE: A missile discharged from a handgun, rifle or cannon., ie. the bullet or cannonball.

QUARRYMEN: Men who work in an excavation from which stone is taken by drilling, blasting, cutting or the like.

QUARTERS: Lodgings for military personnel.

RAKE: A toothed implement for drawing loose material such as ashes or klinkers out of a hot shot furnace.

RAMMER: A long pole with a round metal disc at the head for driving cannon balls, explosive packs and wadding into a gun barrel.

RAMPART: The embankment surrounding a

fort on which the parapet is raised.

RIFLED: A spirally grooved bore of a firearm which causes the projectile to rotate thereby allowing it to travel farther and faster.

RODMAN: Inventor of the Rodman process of cannon manufacturing. T. J. Rodman, Major, U. S. Army.

SABOT: A shoe with a wooden sole and flexible shank used by men working in and around a powder magazine so as not to cause a spark. A term used in construction projects referring to a wooden structure similar to a pallet which is used to store materials off the ground or floor.

SCARP: An embankment or wall at the outer part of a fortification.

SEACOAST GUN: Large cannons used to guard harbor defenses and coastal installations.

SHELL: A hollow, metal projectile filled with an explosive chemical.

SHOT: A solid missile, as a ball of iron, discharged from any firearm.

SHOT FORK: A round, iron double-tined implement used to remove hot cannon balls from the hot shot furnace.

SHOT LADLE: Unit made from metal and formed with an iron ring with the ring's interior bevelled to fit the size cannon ball being carried. The ladle has two arms fitted with wooden handles.

SHOT RASP: A large, course-toothed file used to rub scales which form on cannon balls when they are overheated.

SHOT TONGS: An implement with circular jaws for grasping and lifting cannon balls.

SIEGE GUN: Any cannon used for rapid fire.

SMITH: Nichname or slang given to a blacksmith. Also referred to as a Smithy.

SMOOTHBORE: A firearm without riflings or inner barrel grooves.

TEAMSTER: A person who drives teams of horses or oxen.

TORPEDOES: The old military name given all floating mines. When the submarine was invented capable of discharging a propelled torpedo from underwateer at an enemy vessel, the name torpedo was given exclusively to these weapons and all types of submerged mines were referred to as simply floating mines.

TOUCHHOLE: The orifice in an old cannon through which the powder was ignited.

TRAVERSE: To turn or to swivel to the right or left. In cannon language, the curved metal strip on which a cannon's wheels rode to swing it from side to side.

TROOPS: A body or group of military personnel.

TROUGH: A long, narrow, open receptacle holding any fluid, such as the drainage ditch around a fort.

VENT: A small opening for the passage of gases in a firearm.

WAD or WADDING: Materials used to pack cannon balls and explosive charges in cannon barrels and old black powder rifles. Usually made from pressed dry hay for solid or shell missiles, or good clay for hot shot missiles in cannon and cut cloth for rifles and/or pistols.

WHARF: A wooden or masonry structure erected on the shore of a river or harbor which ships use for loading or unloading stores or people.

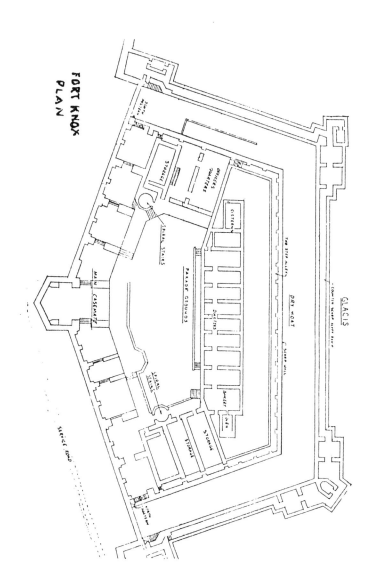

FORT KNOX
PLAN

BIBLIOGRAPHY

It would be impossible to list all the documents necessary in any research of Fort Knox. However, there will be students of historical sites, military history, town, county, and state history, plus genealogists, historians and technical researchers who may wish to *dig* into the files to write more about this magnificent fortification and its builders. Many documents will be found at the National Archives, and to do a thorough research project one would have to spend at least two weeks in the Nation's Capitol. Other documents were found in the Center for Military History; U.S. Army; the Office of Naval History; the National Oceanic and Atmospheric Administration; U.S. Army Corps of Engineers; U.S. Army Military History Institution; the Connecticut State Library; and the State of Maine Parks Commission. There were other sources from which smaller *tidbits* of information were secured, but the majority of these items dealt with the life of Ordnance Sergeant Leopold Hegyi.

(1). Abbot, Henry L., LTC. Report Upon Experiments and Investigations to Develop a System of Submarine Mines for Defending the Harbors of the United States: Professional Papers of the Corps of Engineers, No. 23., Washington, D.C.: GPO, 1881, with Addendas I and II, dated 1882 and 1884.

(2). Adjutant General's Office: Returns, 1841: General Order #6, 1849; General Order #231, 1864; and Reservation Files.

(3). Adjuntant General's Office, Connecticut Men in the Army and Marine Corps of the United States in the Spanish-American War; Hartford, Connecticut: 1919.

(4). Bucknill, John T., Submarine Mines and Torpedoes as Applied to Harbour Defence. New York: John Wiley & Sons, 1889.

(5). Congressional Documents: Statutes at Large, 27th Congress, 3rd Session; Book #1136, 40th Congress, 2nd Session; Book #1291; and Volume 8, #1321, 43rd Congress, 1st Session.

(6). Drake, S. A., Nooks and Corners of the New England Coast, New York: Harper & Bros., 1875.

(7). Dunnack, H. E., Maine Forts, Augusta, Maine: Nash & Sons, 1921.

(8). Hamersly, T., General Register of the United States Army, Washington, D.C., 1882

(9). House of Representatives, Executive Documents: 32nd Congress; 33rd Congress; 35th Congress; 39th Congress; 40th Congress; 41st Congress; 43rd Congress, and the 47th Congress.

(10). Jacques, W. H., Lt., Torpedoes for National Defence. New York: G. P. Putnam's Sons, 1886.

(11). Metcalf, B., (Capt.) Ordnance and Gunnery, U. S. M. A., New York: John Wiley & Sons, 1891.

(12). Niles National Register, Philadelphia, PA.: Volumes 66, 67, and 75.

(13). Reports of the Chief of Engineers: 1844 to 1869.

(14). Reports of the Inspector General: 1869 to 1900.

(15). Reports of the Quartermaster General: 1863 to 1900.

(16). Reports of the Secretary of War: Executive Documents #1163, 40th Congress; Volume 2, 43rd Congress, 1st Session; Report Book #1191; and the Secretary's Report 1860 - 1869; 1873; 1876 - 1878; and 1898 - 1902.

(17). Senate Executive Documents: #1, 28th Congress, 2nd Session; and #190, 47th Congress, 1st Session.

(18). Stotherd, R. H., (Maj.), Notes on Torpedoes, Offensive and Defensive. Washington, D.C.: GPO, 1872.

(19). U. S. Army, Instruction for Field Artillery, Philadelphia, PA.: J. B. Lippencott & Co., 1860.

(20). ———, Ordnance Manual, Washington, D.C.: USGPO, 1860.

Rifle Gallery and Dry Moat. Men were positioned behind these narrow slits and fired their rifles at oncoming enemy troops.

ABOUT THE AUTHOR

John E. Cayford, author, lecturer, historian and educator, is a native of the State of Maine who attended the University of Wisconsin (USAFI), and the University of Maine at Orono, majoring in journalism and science. During the Korean War, he served as an Armed Forces Newsman supplying news articles to U.S. newspapers as well as 26 foreign countries. Upon completion of his military service, he resumed his career as a professional diver, and joined the 1st. Underwater Engineering Unit, USMCD, as the Executive Officer and Chief Diving Officer. At the height of the conflict in Vietnam, he resumed his military service in 1964 serving as an officer onboard a cable laying vessel and on highly classified missile ships with the US Navy's MSTS.

As the president of International Undersea Services, a marine contracting and consulting firm, his underwater work was varied and complex. He authored the semi-technical marine manuals *Underwater Work* and *Underwater Logging,* published by Cornell Maritime Press, and *Diving In Construction Operations* for the U.S.Navy and the National Safety Council, and the *How To Book of Skin and Scuba Diving,* by the Fawcett Company, plus numerous technical articles about the underwater field.

Cayford has been interested in the history of the State of Maine and its maritime history for over

30 years and has written numerous articles about diving, shipping and history. His *Maine's Hall of Fame* articles have been edited and volume 1 is published. Volume 2 of *Maine's Hall of Fame* has been completed and is being readied for printing. Work on Volume 3 has started. He hopes to collect sufficient information to complete 10 *Maine's Hall of Fame* volumes about Maine-born people and their accomplishments.

He lectures throughout the State of Maine on his volumes. He is the author of 18 books, and his articles have appeared in such magazines as: American Heritage; Down East; Sea Classics; Muzzle Blasts; New England Galaxy; Mother Earth News; Skin Diver; Underwater World; World Wood; Today Magazine, and many others.

Cayford is an active member of the Smithsonian and Naval History Foundations, Washington, D.C.; North American Society of Oceanic History; Maine Divers Association, Technical Advisor and past president; National Divers Association, Technical Advisor; Brewer (Maine) Library Corporation, Vice-President and past president, and the Brewer (Maine) Historical Society, Founding Member and past president. He is also a contributor to the Technical Division of the Encyclopedia Brittannia.

MAINE'S
HALL of FAME
VOL. 1

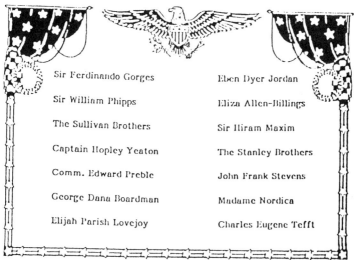

Sir Ferdinando Gorges	Eben Dyer Jordan
Sir William Phipps	Eliza Allen-Billings
The Sullivan Brothers	Sir Hiram Maxim
Captain Hopley Yeaton	The Stanley Brothers
Comm. Edward Preble	John Frank Stevens
George Dana Boardman	Madame Nordica
Elijah Parish Lovejoy	Charles Eugene Tefft

JOHN E. CAYFORD

6x9 size.   208 pps.   Illustrated.   Bibliography.
Hard Cover $17.50   ISBN 0-941216-23-3
Soft Cover $10.00   ISBN 0-941216-22-5

DEMCO